A FULL RANGE OF
BLACK AMERICAN POETRY

"The claim of *THE BLACK POETS* to being at least a partially definitive anthology is that it presents the full range of Black American poetry, from the slave songs to the present day. It is important that folk poetry be included because it is the root and inspiration of later, literary poetry.

"Not only does this book present the full range of Black poetry, but it presents most poets in depth, and in some cases presents aspects of a poet neglected or overlooked before. Gwendolyn Brooks is represented not only by poems on racial and domestic themes, but is revealed as a writer of superb love lyrics.

"Turning away from White models and returning to their roots has freed Black poets to create a new poetry. This book records their progress."
—from the Introduction by Dudley Randall

THE BLACK POETS
Dudley Randall, Editor

BANTAM BOOKS
TORONTO • NEW YORK • LONDON • SYDNEY • AUCKLAND

RL 6, IL age 14 and up

THE BLACK POETS
A Bantam Book / December 1971
12 printings through May 1988

All rights reserved.
Copyright © 1971 by Dudley Randall

ISBN 0-553-27563-1

Contents

Introduction

In 1962 Rosey E. Pool published *Beyond the Blues* in England, a book which was the first comprehensive anthology of black poetry since Langston Hughes's and Arna Bontemps's *The Poetry of the Negro 1746–1949*. Because the United States would have been its greatest market, she tried to find a publisher or a jobber to distribute the book here. Everyone she queried said the book was too special and declined to handle it. Now, in 1970, after Watts and Detroit, and the Black Arts movement, there are so many anthologies of black poetry that each editor must justify the publication of a new one.

I hoped to make *The Black Poets* the definitive anthology of black poetry, but I was shaken when Everett Hoagland sent me his *Black Velvet*, a book I liked so much that I immediately selected poems from it for the anthology. I had been unaware of Hoagland. I wondered how many other good poets I was omitting from the anthology. The inclusion of new poets omitted from previous anthologies is one reason for a new one.

There have been criticisms of the number of new anthologies, but I think they are necessary because each editor may have knowledge of some poet or poets of whom other editors are ignorant. At some future time an editor may cull the best poetry from these anthologies, but for the present, each book is valuable for its new discoveries, and its omissions are compensated for by the inclusions of other anthologies.

To glance down the list: Imamu Amiri Baraka's (LeRoi Jones's) and Larry Neal's *Black Fire* presents many of the younger poets, but it leaves out the two best living black poets, Robert Hayden and Gwendolyn Brooks. If you say that their aim was to present only the younger poets, what about the omission of Don L. Lee and Etheridge Knight, surely two of the best younger poets? Clarence

Major's *The New Black Poetry* has many poets, but they are represented by only one poem each, and we don't get the full range and flavor of their work. Baird Shuman's *Nine Black Poets* gives poets in depth, but is limited in the number. Adam Miller's *Dice or Black Bones* gives good and welcome representation to West Coast poets, but only scanty representation to midwestern ones. Because of these lacks in each anthology, I say the more the better, and some day in the future they will contribute to one definitive anthology.

The claim of *The Black Poets* to being at least a partially definitive anthology is that it presents the full range of black American poetry, from the slave songs to the present day. It is important that folk poetry be included because it is the root and inspiration of later, literary poetry. Folk and ballad poetry influence is seen in Hayden's "The Ballad of Nat Turner," Melvin B. Tolson's "The Birth of John Henry," and in Etheridge Knight's version of the legend of Shine, the stoker on the *Titanic*. In *Black Fire*, Larry Neal gives a different version of the legend.

It is important that the reader, as well as young black poets, be familiar with these roots of black poetry, so that he can recognize them as they recur in Tolson, Sterling A. Brown, Margaret Walker, or in some new young poet of today, and so that the poets can utilize them in their own poetry.

Not only does this book present the full range of black poetry, but it presents most poets in depth, and in some cases presents aspects of a poet neglected or overlooked before. Claude McKay is well-known for his poetry of defiance and rebellion, but some of his later introspective, self-questioning poems, after he was converted from atheism to Catholicism, are included here. Hayden is often characterized (wrongly) as an art for art's sake poet, but some of his poems in this book are the most powerful presentations of the black experience. Frank Horne is best known for his "Letters Found Near a Suicide." Students in my class were so fond of them that I asked them whether they were death-wish oriented. But his later poetry, when he was struggling for strength after paralysis, is included here. Gwendolyn Brooks is represented not only by poems on racial and domestic themes, but is revealed as a writer of superb love lyrics.

In addition, new poets, or poets seldom anthologized before, are included, such as Everett Hoagland, James Randall, Jr., Stephany, Carolyn M. Rodgers, Doughtry Long, and Johari Amini.

The first literary black poets tried to write as whites for a white audience. Phillis Wheatley imitated Pope and Dryden. Their models were likely to be genteel or to antedate the current poetic practices. In the Harlem Renaissance, Countee Cullen wrote under the influence of Keats and Housman, and Claude McKay wrote sonnets in the tradition of Wordsworth and Milton. It took the impingement of racism on Cullen's life, and McKay's belligerent personality, to give their poetry distinction. Only Langston Hughes and Jean Toomer, one by his use of colloquial black speech and blues form, and the other by his employment of new images and symbolism, were abreast of the poetic practices of the day.

In the post-Renaissance generation, Sterling A. Brown and Margaret Walker continued Hughes's use of folk materials, and Robert Hayden, Gwendolyn Brooks, Melvin B. Tolson, and Margaret Danner brought black poetry abreast of its time by absorbing and mastering the techniques of T. S. Eliot, Hart Crane, Ezra Pound.

The poets of the sixties and seventies have gone further than the poets of the post-Renaissance. The best of them have absorbed the techniques of the masters, have rejected them, and have gone in new directions. Perhaps this rejection had its roots in the movement of the fifties and sixties. When the poets saw the contorted faces of the mobs, saw officers of the law commit murder, and "respectable" people scheme to break the law (there was no cry for law and order then), perhaps they asked themselves, Why should we seek to be integrated with such a society? Perhaps they resolved to work toward a more civilized, a more humane society.

This alienation from white society initiated a turning away from its values and its poetry. Poets turned to poetry of the folk, of the streets, to jazz musicians, to the language of black people for their models. Their first impulse was no longer to send a poem to *Poetry Magazine* or *Harper's*, but to think of *Black World, Journal of Black Poetry, Black Dialogue, Soulbook, Freedomways,* or *Liberator*. This emancipation from white literary models and critics freed them to create a new black poetry of their own. Such freedom was necessary if they were to create a truly original poetry. This is not to say that they remained ignorant of the currents of contemporary poetry, but that their attitude toward it was different. What they could use, they took, but they wrote as black men, not as black writers trying to be white. They tried to change language, to turn it around, to give new meanings and connotations to words. One example of this is the word *black*, which no longer connotes evil or dirt, but pride and beauty.

Examples of their success in "blackening the language" are phrases that have passed into common speech and that one repeats without knowing the originator, such as Imamu Baraka's (LeRoi Jones's) "up against the wall" and "black art," and Don Lee's "think black," "black pride," "the unpeople," "the realpeople," "the world-runners," "I under/overstand," "blackwriting," "integration of negroes with black people," and "talking black and sleeping white."

This turning away from white models and returning to their roots has freed black poets to create a new poetry. This book records their progress. They no longer imitate white models, strain toward white magazines, defer to white critics, or court white readers. They are in the process of creating a new literature. Whatever the outcome, they are taking care of business.

DUDLEY RANDALL

FOLK POETRY

Walk Together Children

Walk together children,
Don't you get weary,
Walk together children,
Don't you get weary.
Oh, talk together children,
Don't you get weary,
There's a great camp meeting in the Promised Land.

Sing together children,
Don't you get weary,
Sing together children,
Don't you get weary.
Oh, shout together children,
Don't you get weary,
There's a great camp meeting in the Promised Land.

Gwineter mourn and never tire,
Mourn and never tire,
Mourn and never tire.
There's a great camp meeting in the Promised Land.

Oh, get you ready children,
Don't you get weary,
Get you ready children,
Don't you get weary.
We'll enter there, oh, children,
Don't you get weary,
There's a great camp meeting in the Promised Land.

This Sun is Hot

Dis sun are hot,
Dis hoe are heavy,
Dis grass grow furder dan I can reach;
An' as I looks
At dis Cotton fiel',
I thinks I mus' 'a' been called to preach.

That Hypocrite

I tell you how dat hypocrite do,
He come down to my house, an' talk about you;
He talk about me, an' he talk about you;
An' dat's de way dat hypocrite do.

I tell you how dat hypocrite pray.
He pray out loud in de hypocrite way.
He pray out loud, got a heap to say;
An' dat's de way dat hypocrite pray.

I tell you how dat hypocrite 'ten',
He 'ten' dat he love, an' he don't love men.
He 'ten' dat he love, an' he hate Br'er Ben;
An' dat's de way dat hypocrite 'ten'.

Old Man Know-All

Ole man Know-All, he come 'round
Wid his nose in de air, turned 'way frum de ground.
His ole woolly head hain't been combed fer a week;
It say: "Keep still, while Know-All speak."

Ole man Know-All's tongue, it run;
He jes know'd ev'rything under de sun.
When you knowed one thing, he knowed mo'.
He 'us sharp 'nough to stick an' green 'nough to grow.

Ole man Know-All died las' week.
He got drowned in de middle o' de creek.
De bridge wus dar, an' dar to stay.
But he knowed too much to go dat way.

Raise a "Rucus" To-Night

Two liddle Niggers all dressed in white, (Raise a rucus
to-night.)
Want to go to Heaben on de tail of a kite. (Raise a rucus
to-night.)
De kite string broke; dem Niggers fell; (Raise a rucus to-
night.)
Whar dem Niggers go, I hain't gwineter tell. (Raise a
rucus to-night.)

A Nigger an' a w'ite man a playin' seben up; (Raise a
rucus to-night.)
De Nigger beat de w'ite man, but 'e's skeered to pick it
up. (Raise a rucus to-night.)
Dat Nigger grabbed de money, an' de w'ite man fell.
(Raise a rucus to-night.)
How de Nigger run, I'se not gwineter, tell. (Raise a rucus
to-night.)

Look here, Nigger! Let me tell you a naked fac': (Raise
a rucus to-night.)
You mought a been cullud widout bein' dat black; (Raise
a rucus to-night.)
Dem 'ar feet look lak youse sho' walkin' back; (Raise a
rucus to-night.)
An' yo' ha'r, it look lak a chyarpet tack. (Raise a rucus
to-night.)

>   Oh come 'long, chilluns, come 'long,
>   W'ile dat moon are shinin' bright.
>   Let's git on board, an' float down de river,
>   An' raise dat rucus to-night.

• I'll Wear Me a Cotton Dress

Oh, will you wear red? Oh, will you wear red?
Oh, will you wear red, Milly Biggers?
"I won't wear red,
It's too much lak Missus' head.
I'll wear me a cotton dress,
Dyed wid copperse an' oak-bark."

Oh, will you wear blue? Oh, will you wear blue?
Oh, will you wear blue, Milly Biggers?
"I won't wear blue,
It's too much lak Missus' shoe.
I'll wear me a cotton dress,
Dyed wid copperse an' oak-bark."

You sholy would wear gray? You sholy would wear gray?
You sholy would wear gray, Milly Biggers?
"I won't wear gray,
It's too much lak Missus' way.
I'll wear me a cotton dress,
Dyed wid copperse an' oak-bark."

Well, will you wear white? Well, will you wear white?
Well, will you wear white, Milly Biggers?
"I won't wear white,
I'd get dirty long 'fore night.
I'll wear me a cotton dress,
Dyed wid copperse an' oak-bark."

Now, will you wear black? Now, will you wear black?
Now, will you wear black, Milly Biggers?
"I mought wear black,
Case it's de color o' my back;
An' it looks lak my cotton dress,
Dyed wid copperse* an' oak-bark."

---

* Copperse is copperas, or sulphate of iron.

John Henry

When John Henry was a little fellow,
    You could hold him in the palm of your hand,
He said to his pa, "When I grow up
    I'm gonna be a steel-driving man.
        Gonna be a steel-driving man."

When John Henry was a little baby,
    Setting on his mammy's knee,
He said "The Big Bend Tunnel on the C. & O. Road
    Is gonna be the death of me,
        Gonna be the death of me."

One day his captain told him,
    How he had bet a man
That John Henry would beat his steam drill down,
    Cause John Henry was the best in the land,
        John Henry was the best in the land.

John Henry kissed his hammer,
    White man turned on steam,
Shaker held John Henry's trusty steel,
    Was the biggest race the world had ever seen,
        Lord, biggest race the world ever seen.

John Henry on the right side
    The steam drill on the left,
"Before I'll let your steam drill beat me down,
    I'll hammer my fool self to death,
        Hammer my fool self to death."

John Henry walked in the tunnel,
    His captain by his side,
The mountain so tall, John Henry so small,
    He laid down his hammer and he cried,
        Laid down his hammer and he cried.

Captain heard a mighty rumbling,
    Said "The mountain must be caving in,

John Henry said to the captain,
  "It's my hammer swinging in de wind,
    My hammer swinging in de wind."

John Henry said to his shaker,
  "Shaker, you'd better pray;
For if ever I miss this piece of steel,
  Tomorrow'll be your burial day,
    Tomorrow'll be your burial day."

John Henry said to his shaker,
  "Lordy, shake it while I sing,
I'm pulling my hammer from my shoulders down,
  Great Gawdamighty, how she ring,
    Great Gawdamighty, how she ring!"

John Henry said to his captain,
  "Before I ever leave town,
Gimme one mo' drink of dat tom-cat gin,
  And I'll hammer dat steam driver down,
    I'll hammer dat steam driver down."

John Henry said to his captain,
  "Before I ever leave town,
Gimme a twelve-pound hammer wid a whale-bone handle,
  And I'll hammer dat steam driver down,
    I'll hammer dat steam drill on down."

John Henry said to his captain,
  "A man ain't nothin' but a man,
But before I'll let dat steam drill beat me down,
  I'll die wid my hammer in my hand,
    Die wid my hammer in my hand."

The man that invented the steam drill
  He thought he was mighty fine,
John Henry drove down fourteen feet,
  While the steam drill only made nine,
    Steam drill only made nine.

"Oh, lookaway over yonder, captain,
    You can't see like me,"
He gave a long and loud and lonesome cry,
    "Lawd, a hammer be the death of me,
        A hammer be the death of me!"

John Henry had a little woman,
    Her name was Polly Ann,
John Henry took sick, she took his hammer,
    She hammered like a natural man,
        Lawd, she hammered like a natural man.

John Henry hammering on the mountain
    As the whistle blew for half-past two,
The last words his captain heard him say,
    "I've done hammered my insides in two,
        Lawd, I've hammered my insides in two."

The hammer that John Henry swung
    It weighed over twelve pound,
He broke a rib in his left hand side
    And his intrels fell on the ground,
        And his intrels fell on the ground.

John Henry, O, John Henry,
    His blood is running red,
Fell right down with his hammer to the ground,
    Said, "I beat him to the bottom but I'm dead,
        Lawd, beat him to the bottom but I'm dead."

When John Henry was laying there dying,
    The people all by his side,
The very last words they heard him say,
    "Give me a cool drink of water 'fore I die,
        Cool drink of water 'fore I die."

John Henry had a little woman,
    The dress she wore was red,
She went down the track, and she never looked back,
    Going where her man fell dead,
        Going where her man fell dead.

John Henry had a little woman,
   The dress she wore was blue,
De very last words she said to him,
    "John Henry, I'll be true to you,
      John Henry, I'll be true to you."

"Who's gonna shoes yo' little feet,
   Who's gonna glove yo' hand,
Who's gonna kiss yo' pretty, pretty cheek,
    Now you done lost yo' man?
      Now you done lost yo' man?"

"My mammy's gonna shoes my little feet,
   Pappy gonna glove my hand,
My sister's gonna kiss my pretty, pretty cheek,
    Now I done lost my man,
      Now I done lost my man."

They carried him down by the river,
   And buried him in the sand,
And everybody that passed that way,
    Said, "There lies that steel-driving man,
      There lies a steel-driving man."

They took John Henry to the river,
   And buried him in the sand,
And every locomotive come a-roaring by,
    Says "There lies that steel-drivin' man,
      Lawd, there lies a *steel*-drivin' man."

Some say he came from Georgia,
   And some from Alabam,
But it's wrote on the rock at the Big Bend Tunnel,
    That he was an East Virginia man,
      Lord, Lord, an East Virginia man.

She Hugged Me and Kissed Me

I see'd her in de Springtime,
I see'd her in de Fall,
I see'd her in de Cotton patch,
A cameing from de Ball.

She hug me, an' she kiss me,
She wrung my han' an' cried.
She said I wus de sweetes' thing
Dat ever lived or died.

She hug me an' she kiss me.
Oh Heaben! De touch o' her han'!
She said I wus de puttiest thing
In de shape o' mortal man.

I told her dat I love her,
Dat my love wus bed-cord strong;
Den I axed her w'en she'd have me,
An' she jes say "Go long!"

Slave Marriage Ceremony Supplement

Dark an' stormy may come de wedder;
I jines dis he-male an' dis she-male togedder.
Let none, but Him dat makes de thunder,
Put dis he-male an' dis she-male asunder.
I darfore 'nounce you bofe de same.
Be good, go 'long, an' keep up yo' name.
De broomstick's jumped, de worl's not wide.
She's now yo' own. Salute yo' bride!

Blessing Without Company

Oh Lawd have mussy now upon us,
An' keep 'way some our neighbors from us.
For w'en dey all comes down upon us,
Dey eats mos' all our victuals from us.

The Old Section Boss

I once knowed an ole Sexion Boss but he done been laid
low.
I once knowed an ole Sexion Boss but he done been laid
low.
He "Caame frum gude ole Ireland some fawhrty year
ago."

W'en I ax 'im fer a job, he say: "Nayger, w'at can yer do?"
W'en I ax 'im fer a job, he say: "Nayger, w'at can yer do?"
"I can line de track; tote de jack, de pick an' shovel too."

Says he: "Nayger, de railroad's done, an' de chyars is on
de track,"
Says he: "Nayger, de railroad's done, an' de chyars is on
de track,"
"Transportation brung yer here, but yo' money'll take yer
back."

I went down to de Deepo, an' my ticket I sho' did draw.
I went down to de Deepo, an' my ticket I sho' did draw.
To take me over dat ole Iron Mountain to de State o'
Arkansaw.

As I went sailin' down de road, I met my mudder-in-law.
I wus so tired an' hongry, man, dat I couldn' wuk my jaw.
Fer I hadn't had no decent grub since I lef' ole Arkansaw.

Her bread wus hard corndodgers; dat meat, I couldn'
chaw.
Her bread wus hard corndodgers; dat meat, I couldn'
chaw.
You see; dat's de way de Hoosiers feeds way out in
Arkansaw.

The Turtle's Song

Mud turkle settin' on de end of a log,
A-watchin' of a tadpole a-turnin' to a frog.
He sees Br'er B'ar a-pullin' lak a mule.
He sees Br'er Tearpin a-makin' him a fool.

Br'er B'ar pull de rope an' he puff an' he blow;
But he cain't git de Tearpin out'n de water from below.
Dat big clay root is a-holdin' dat rope,
Br'er Tearpin's got 'im fooled, an' dere hain't no hope.

Mud turkle settin' on de end o' dat log;
Sing fer de tadpole a-turnin' to a frog,
Sing to Br'er B'ar a-pullin' lak a mule,
Sing to Br'er Tearpin a-makin' 'im a fool:—

"Oh, Br'er Rabbit! Yo' eyes mighty big!"
"Yes, Br'er Turkle! Dey're made fer to see."
"Oh, Br'er Tearpin! Yo' house mighty cu'ous!"
"Yes, Br'er Turkle, but it jest suits me."

"Oh, Br'er B'ar! You pulls mighty stout."
"Yes, Br'er Turkle! Dat's right smart said!"
"Right, Br'er B'ar! Dat sounds bully good,
But you'd oughter git a liddle mo' pull in de head."

Chuck Will's Widow Song

Oh nimber, nimber Will-o!
My crooked, crooked bill-o!
I'se settin' down right now, on
    de sweet pertater hill-o.

Oh nimber, nimber Will-o!
My crooked, crooked bill-o!
Two liddle naked babies, my two
    brown aigs now fill-o.

Oh nimber, nimber Will-o!
My crooked, crooked bill-o!
Don't hurt de liddle babies; dey
    is too sweet to kill-o.

Spirituals

No More Auction Block

No more auction block for me,
No more, no more,
No more auction block for me,
Many thousand gone.

No more peck of corn for me,
No more, no more,
No more peck of corn for me,
Many thousand gone.

No more pint of salt for me,
No more, no more,
No more pint of salt for me,
Many thousand gone.

No more driver's lash for me,
No more, no more,
No more driver's lash for me,
Many thousand gone.

I Know de Moonlight

I know de moonlight, I know de starlight,
I lay dis body down.
I walk in de moonlight, I walk in de starlight,
To lay dis body down.
I lie in de grave and stretch out my arms,
I lay dis body down.
I go to de Judgment in de evenin' of de day,
When I lay dis body down,
And my soul and yo' soul will meet in de day
When I lay dis body down.

Go Down, Moses

Go down, Moses,
Way down in Egyptland
Tell old Pharaoh
To let my people go.

When Israel was in Egyptland
Let my people go
Oppressed so hard they could not stand
Let my people go.

Go down, Moses,
Way down in Egyptland
Tell old Pharaoh
"Let my people go."

"Thus saith the Lord," bold Moses said,
"Let my people go;
If not I'll smite your first-born dead
Let my people go.

"No more shall they in bondage toil,
Let my people go;
Let them come out with Egypt's spoil,
Let my people go."

The Lord told Moses what to do
Let my people go;
To lead the children of Israel through,
Let my people go.

Go down, Moses,
Way down in Egyptland,
Tell old Pharaoh,
"Let my people go!"

Joshua Fit De Battle of Jericho

Joshua fit de battle of Jericho,
Jericho, Jericho,
Joshua fit de battle of Jericho,
And de walls come tumbling down.

You may talk about yo' king of Gideon
Talk about yo' man of Saul,
Dere's none like good old Joshua
At de battle of Jericho.

Up to de walls of Jericho,
He marched with spear in hand;
"Go blow dem ram horns," Joshua cried,
"Kase de battle am in my hand."

Den de lamb ram sheep horns begin to blow,
Trumpets begin to sound,
Joshua commanded de chillen to shout,
And de walls come tumbling down.

Dat morning,
Joshua fit de battle of Jericho,
Jericho, Jericho,
Joshua fit de battle of Jericho,
And de walls come tumbling down.

Dere's No Hidin' Place Down Dere

Dere's no hidin' place down dere,
Dere's no hidin' place down dere.

O I went to de rock to hide my face,
De rock cried out, "No hidin' place,"
Dere's no hidin' place down dere.

Oh de rock cried, "I'm burnin' too,"
Oh de rock cried, "I'm burnin' too,"
Oh de rock cried out I'm burnin' too,
I want a go to hebben as well as you,
Dere's no hidin' place down dere.

Oh de sinner man he gambled an' fell,
Oh de sinner man he gambled an' fell,
Oh de sinner man gambled, he gambled an' fell;
He wanted to go to hebben, but he had to go to hell,
Dere's no hidin' place down dere.

I Got a Home in Dat Rock

I got a home in dat rock,
Don't you see?
I got a home in dat rock,
Don't you see?
Between de earth an' sky,
Thought I heard my Saviour cry,
You got a home in dat rock,
Don't you see?

Poor man Laz'rus, poor as I,
Don't you see?
Poor man Laz'rus, poor as I,
Don't you see?
Poor man Laz'rus, poor as I,
When he died he found a home on high,
He had a home in dat rock,
Don't you see?

Rich man Dives, he lived so well,
Don't you see?
Rich man Dives, he lived so well,
Don't you see?
Rich man Dives, he lived so well,
When he died he found a home in Hell,
He had no home in dat rock,
Don't you see?

God gave Noah de Rainbow sign,
Don't you see?
God gave Noah de Rainbow sign,
Don't you see?
God gave Noah de Rainbow sign,
No more water but fire next time,
Better get a home in dat rock,
Don't you see?

Deep River

Deep river, my home is over Jordan,
Deep river, Lord; I want to cross over into camp ground.

O children, O, don't you want to go to that gospel feast,
That promised land, that land, where all is peace?

Deep river, my home is over Jordan,
Deep river, Lord; I want to cross over into camp ground.

Steal Away to Jesus

Steal away, steal away, steal away to Jesus,
Steal away, steal away home,
I ain't got long to stay here.

My Lord, He calls me,
He calls me by the thunder,
The trumpet sounds within-a my soul,
I ain't got long to stay here.

Steal away, steal away, steal away to Jesus,
Steal away, steal away home,
I ain't got long to stay here.

Green trees a-bending,
Po' sinner stands a-trembling,
The trumpet sounds within-a my soul,
I ain't got long to stay here.

Steal away, steal away, steal away to Jesus,
Steal away, steal away home,
I ain't got long to stay here.

Git on Board, Little Chillen

Git on board, little chillen,
Git on board, little chillen,
Git on board, little chillen,
Dere's room for many a mo'.

De gospel train's a-comin',
I hear it jus' at han',
I hear de car wheels movin',
An' rumblin' through de lan'.

Git on board, little chillen,
Git on board, little chillen,
Git on board, little chillen,
Dere's room for many a mo'.

De fare is cheap, an' all can go,
De rich an' poor are dere,
No second class aboard dis train,
No diffrunce in de fare.

Git on board, little chillen,
Git on board, little chillen,
Git on board, little chillen,
Dere's room for many a mo'.

Give Me Jesus

Oh, when I come to die,
Oh, when I come to die,
Oh, when I come to die,
Give me Jesus.
In dat mornin' when I rise,
Dat mornin' when I rise,
In dat mornin' when I rise,
Give me Jesus.

Give me Jesus, give me Jesus,
You may have all dis worl', give me Jesus,
Oh, give me Jesus, give me Jesus,
You may have all dis worl', give me Jesus.

Dark midnight was my cry,
Dark midnight was my cry,
Dark midnight was my cry,
Give me Jesus.
I heard a mourner say,
I heard a mourner say,
I heard a mourner say,
Give me Jesus.

What Yo' Gwine to do when Yo' Lamp Burn Down?

O, po' sinner, O, now is yo' time,
O, po' sinner, O, what yo' gwine to do when yo' lamp burn
   down?

Fin' de Eas', fin' de Wes',
What yo' gwine to do when yo' lamp burn down?
Fire gwine to burn down de wilderness,
What yo' gwine to do when yo' lamp burn down?

Head got wet wid de midnight dew,
What yo' gwine to do when yo' lamp burn down?
Mornin' star was a witness too,
What yo' gwine to do when yo' lamp burn down?

Dey whipped Him up an' dey whipped Him down,
What yo' gwine to do when yo' lamp burn down?
Dey whipped dat man all ovah town,
What yo' gwine to do when yo' lamp burn down.

Dey nailed His han' an' dey nailed His feet,
What yo' gwine to do when yo' lamp burn down?
De hammer was heard on Jerusalem street,
What yo' gwine to do when yo' lamp burn down?

Crucifixion

They crucified my Lord, an' He never said a mumbalin'
   word;
They crucified my Lord, an' He never said a mumbalin'
   word.
Not a word, not a word, not a word.

They nailed Him to the tree, an' He never said a mum-
   balin' word;
They nailed Him to the tree, an' He never said a mum-
   balin' word.
Not a word, not a word, not a word.

They pierced Him in the side, an' He never said a mumbalin' word,
They pierced Him in the side, an' He never said a mumbalin' word.
Not a word, not a word, not a word.

The blood came twinklin' down, an' He never said a mumbalin' word,
The blood came twinklin' down, an' He never said a mumbalin' word.
Not a word, not a word, not a word.

He bowed His head an' died, an' He never said a mumbalin' word,
He bowed His head an' died, an' He never said a mumbalin' word.
Not a word, not a word, not a word.

Were You There when They Crucified My Lord?

Were you there, when they crucified my Lord?
Were you there, when they crucified my Lord?
Oh, sometimes, it causes me to tremble, tremble, tremble.
Where you there, when they crucified my Lord?

Were you there, when they nailed him to the tree?
Were you there, when they nailed him to the tree?
Oh, sometimes, it causes me to tremble, tremble, tremble.
Were you there, when they nailed him to the tree?

Were you there, when they pierced him in the side?
Were you there, when they pierced him in the side?
Oh, sometimes, it causes me to tremble, tremble, tremble.
Were you there, when they pierced him in the side?

Were you there, when the sun refused to shine?
Were you there, when the sun refused to shine?
Oh, sometimes, it causes me to tremble, tremble, tremble.
Were you there, when the sun refused to shine?

Were you there, when they laid him in the tomb?
Were you there, when they laid him in the tomb?
Oh, sometimes, it causes me to tremble, tremble, tremble.
Were you there, when they laid him in the tomb?

I Thank God I'm Free at Las'

Free at las', free at las',
I thank God I'm free at las'.
Free at las', free at las',
I thank God I'm free at las'.

Way down yonder in de graveyard walk,
I thank God I'm free at las'.
Me an' my Jesus gwineter meet an' talk,
I thank God I'm free at las'.

On-a my knees when de light pass by,
I thank God I'm free at las'.
Thought my soul would arise and fly,
I thank God I'm free at las'.

Some o' dese mornin's bright and fair,
I thank God I'm free at las',
Gwineter meet my Jesus in de middle of de air,
I thank God I'm free at las'.

De Ole Sheep Dey Know De Road

Oh, de ole sheep, dey know de road,
De ole sheep, dey know de road,
De ole sheep, dey know de road,
De young lambs must find de way.

My brother, better mind how you walk on de cross,
    De young lambs must find de way,
For your foot might slip, and yo' soul git lost,
    De young lambs must find de way.

Better mind dat sun, and see how she run,
    De young lambs must find de way,
And mind, don't let her catch you wid yo' work undone,
    De young lambs must find de way.

Oh, de ole sheep, dey know de road,
De ole sheep, dey know de road,
De ole sheep, dey know de road,
Young lambs must find de way.

LITERARY POETRY

Black Poet, White Critic

A critic advises
not to write on controversial subjects
like freedom or murder,
but to treat universal themes
and timeless symbols
like the white unicorn.

A white unicorn?

DUDLEY RANDALL

The Forerunners

from America

America, it is to thee,
Thou boasted land of liberty,—
It is to thee I raise my song,
Thou land of blood, and crime, and wrong.
It is to thee, my native land,
From which has issued many a band
To tear the black man from his soil,
And force him here to delve and toil;
Chained on your blood-bemoistened sod,
Cringing beneath a tyrant's rod,
Stripped of those rights which Nature's God
Bequeathed to all the human race,
Bound to a petty tyrant's nod,
Because he wears a paler face.

JAMES M. WHITFIELD

LUCY TERRY (1730–1821)

Bar's Fight, August 28, 1746

August 'twas, the twenty-fifth,
Seventeen hundred forty-six,
The Indians did in ambush lay,
Some very valient men to slay,
The names of whom I'll not leave out:
Samuel Allen like a hero fout,
And though he was so brave and bold,
His face no more shall we behold;
Eleazer Hawks was killed outright,
Before he had time to fight,
Before he did the Indians see,
Was shot and killed immediately;
Oliver Amsden, he was slain,
Which caused his friends much grief and pain;
Simeon Amsden they found dead,
Not many rods off from his head;
Adonijah Gillet, we do hear,
Did lose his life, which was so dear;
John Saddler fled across the water,
And so escaped the dreadful slaughter;
Eunice Allen see the Indians comeing,
And hoped to save herself by running,
And had not her petticoats stopt her,
The awful creatures had not cotched her,
And tommyhawked her on the head,
And left her on the ground for dead;
Young Samuel Allen, oh! lack-a-day,
Was taken and carried to Canada.

PHILLIS WHEATLEY (c. 1753–94)

from
To the Right Honorable William, Earl of Dartmouth

Should you, my lord, while you pursue my song,
Wonder from whence my love of *Freedom* sprung,
Whence flow these wishes for the common good,
By feeling hearts alone best understood,
I, young in life, by seeming cruel fate
Was snatch'd from *Afric's* fancy'd happy seat:
What pangs excruciating must molest,
What sorrows labour in my parent's breast?
Steel'd was the soul and by no misery mov'd
That from a father seiz'd his babe belov'd.
Such, such my case. And can I then but pray
Others may never feel tyrannic sway?

FRANCES E. W. HARPER (1825–1911)

The Slave Auction

The sale began—young girls were there,
    Defenceless in their wretchedness,
Whose stifled sobs of deep despair
    Revealed their anguish and distress.

And mothers stood with streaming eyes,
    And saw their dearest children sold;
Unheeded rose their bitter cries,
    While tyrants bartered them for gold.

And woman, with her love and truth—
    For these in sable forms may dwell—
Gaz'd on the husband of her youth,
    With anguish none may paint or tell.

And men, whose sole crime was their hue,
    The impress of their Maker's hand,
And frail and shrinking children, too,
    Were gathered in that mournful band.

Ye who have laid your love to rest,
    And wept above their lifeless clay,
Know not the anguish of that breast,
    Whose lov'd are rudely torn away.

Ye may not know how desolate
    Are bosoms rudely forced to part,
And how a dull and heavy weight
    Will press the life-drops from the heart.

Bury Me In a Free Land

Make me a grave where'er you will,
In a lowly plain, or a lofty hill;
Make it among earth's humblest graves,
But not in a land where men are slaves.

I could not rest if around my grave
I heard the steps of a trembling slave;
His shadow above my silent tomb
Would make it a place of fearful gloom.

I could not rest if I heard the tread
Of a coffle gang to the shambles led,
And the mother's shriek of wild despair
Rise like a curse on the trembling air.

I could not sleep if I saw the lash
Drinking her blood at each fearful gash,
And I saw her babes torn from her breast,
Like trembling doves from their parent nest.

I'd shudder and start if I heard the bay
Of bloodhounds seizing their human prey,
And I heard the captive plead in vain
As they bound afresh his galling chain.

If I saw young girls from their mothers' arms
Bartered and sold for their youthful charms,
My eye would flash with a mournful flame,
My death-paled cheek grow red with shame.

I would sleep, dear friends, where bloated might
Can rob no man of his dearest right;
My rest shall be calm in any grave
Where none can call his brother a slave.

I ask no monument, proud and high,
To arrest the gaze of the passers-by;
All that my yearning spirit craves,
Is bury me not in a land of slaves.

JAMES WELDON JOHNSON (1871–1938)

Listen, Lord—A Prayer

O Lord, we come this morning
Knee-bowed and body-bent
Before thy throne of grace.
O Lord—this morning—
Bow our hearts beneath our knees,
And our knees in some lonesome valley.
We come this morning—
Like empty pitchers to a full fountain,
With no merits of our own.
O Lord—open up a window of heaven,
And lean out far over the battlements of glory,
And listen this morning.

Lord, have mercy on proud and dying sinners—
Sinners hanging over the mouth of hell,
Who seem to love their distance well.
Lord—ride by this morning—
Mount your milk-white horse,
And ride-a this morning—
And in your ride, ride by old hell,
Ride by the dingy gates of hell,
And stop poor sinners in their headlong plunge.

And now, O Lord, this man of God,
Who breaks the bread of life this morning—
Shadow him in the hollow of thy hand,
And keep him out of the gunshot of the devil.
Take him, Lord—this morning—
Wash him with hyssop inside and out,
Hang him up and drain him dry of sin.
Pin his ear to the wisdom-post,
And make his words sledge hammers of truth—
Beating on the iron heart of sin.

Lord God, this morning—
Put his eye to the telescope of eternity,
And let him look upon the paper walls of time.
Lord, turpentine his imagination,
Put perpetual motion in his arms,
Fill him full of the dynamite of thy power,
Anoint him all over with the oil of thy salvation,
And set his tongue on fire.

And now, O Lord—
When I've done drunk my last cup of sorrow—
When I've been called everything but a child of God—
When I'm done travelling up the rough side of the
    mountain—
O—Mary's Baby—
When I start down the steep and slippery steps of death—
When this old world begins to rock beneath my feet—
Lower me to my dusty grave in peace
To wait for that great gittin' up morning—Amen.

O Black and Unknown Bards

O black and unknown bards of long ago,
How came your lips to touch the sacred fire?
How, in your darkness, did you come to know
The power and beauty of the minstrel's lyre?
Who first from midst his bonds lifted his eyes?
Who first from out the still watch, lone and long,
Feeling the ancient faith of prophets rise
Within his dark-kept soul, burst into song?

Heart of what slave poured out such melody
As "Steal away to Jesus"? On its strains
His spirit must have nightly floated free,
Though still about his hands he felt his chains.
Who heard great "Jordan roll"? Whose starward eye
Saw chariot "swing low"? And who was he
That breathed that comforting, melodic sigh,
"Nobody knows de trouble I see"?

What merely living clod, what captive thing,
Could up toward God through all its darkness grope,
And find within its deadened heart to sing
These songs of sorrow, love and faith, and hope?
How did it catch that subtle undertone,
That note in music heard not with the ears?
How sound the elusive reed so seldom blown,
Which stirs the soul or melts the heart to tears.

Not that great German master in his dream
Of harmonies that thundered amongst the stars
At the creation, ever heard a theme
Nobler than "Go down, Moses." Mark its bars
How like a mighty trumpet-call they stir
The blood. Such are the notes that men have sung
Going to valorous deeds; such tones there were
That helped make history when Time was young.

There is a wide, wide wonder in it all,
That from degraded rest and servile toil
The fiery spirit of the seer should call
These simple children of the sun and soil.
O black slave singers, gone, forgot, unfamed,
You—you alone, of all the long, long line
Of those who've sung untaught, unknown, unnamed,
Have stretched out upward, seeking the divine.

You sang not deeds of heroes or of kings;
No chant of bloody war, no exulting paean
Of arms-won triumphs; but your humble strings
You touched in chord with music empyrean.
You sang far better than you knew; the songs
That for your listeners' hungry hearts sufficed
Still live,—but more than this to you belongs:
You sang a race from wood and stone to Christ.

PAUL LAURENCE DUNBAR (1872–1906)

An Ante-Bellum Sermon

We is gathahed hyeah, my brothahs,
    In dis howlin' wildaness,
Fu' to speak some words of comfo't
    To each othah in distress.
An' we chooses fu' ouah subjic'
    Dis—we'll 'splain it by an' by;
"An' de Lawd said, 'Moses, Moses,'
    An' de man said, 'Hyeah am I.' "

Now ole Pher'oh, down in Egypt,
    Was de wuss man evah bo'n,
And he had de Hebrew chillun
    Down dah wukin' in his co'n;
'T well de Lawd got tiahed o' his foolin',
    An' sez he: "I'll let him know—
Look hyeah, Moses, go tell Pher'oh
    Fu' to let dem chillun go."

"An' ef he refuse to do it,
    I will make him rue de houah,
Fu' I'll empty down on Egypt
    All de vials of my powah."
Yes, he did—an' Pher'oh's ahmy
    Was n't wuth a ha'f a dime;
Fu' de Lawd will he'p his chillun,
    You kin trust him evah time.

An' yo' enemies may 'sail you
    In de back an' in de front;
But de Lawd is all aroun' you,
    Fu' to ba' de battle's brunt.

Dey kin fo'ge yo' chains an' shackles
    F'om de mountains to de sea;
But de Lawd will sen' some Moses
    Fu' to set his chillun free.

An' de lan' shall hyeah his thundah,
    Lak a blas' f'om Gab'el's ho'n,
Fu' de Lawd of hosts is mighty
    When he girds his ahmor on.
Bu fu' feah some one mistakes me,
    I will pause right hyeah to say,
Dat I'm still a-preachin' ancient,
    I ain't talkin' 'bout to-day.

But I tell you, fellah christuns,
    Things'll happen mighty strange;
Now, de Lawd done dis fu' Isrul,
    An' his ways don't nevah change,
An' de love he showed to Isrul
    Was n't all on Isrul spent;
Now don't run an' tell yo' mastahs
    Dat I's preachin' discontent.

'Cause I is n't; I'se a-judgin'
    Bible people by deir ac's;
I'se a-givin' you de Scriptuah,
    I'se a-handin' you de fac's.
Cose ole Pher'oh b'lieved in slav'ry,
    But de Lawd he let him see,
Dat de people he put bref in,—
    Evah mothah's son was free.

An' dahs othahs thinks lak Pher'oh,
    But dey calls de Scriptuah liar,
Fu' de Bible says "a servant
    Is a-worthy of his hire."
An' you cain't git roun' nor thoo dat,
    An' you cain't git ovah it,
Fu' whatevah place you git in,
    Dis hyeah Bible too'll fit.

So you see de Lawd's intention,
　　Evah sence de worl' began,
Was dat His almighty freedom
　　Should belong to evah man,
But I think it would be bettah,
　　Ef I'd pause agin to say,
Dat I'm talkin' 'bout ouah freedom
　　In a Bibleistic way.

But de Moses is a-comin',
　　An' he's comin', suah and fas'
We kin hyeah his feet a-trompin',
　　We kin hyeah his trumpit blas'.
But I want to wa'n you people,
　　Don't you git too brigity;
An' don't you git to braggin'
　　'Bout dese things, you wait an' see.

But when Moses wif his powah
　　Comes an' sets us chillun free,
We will praise de gracious Mastah
　　Dat has gin us liberty;
An' we'll shout ouah halleluyahs,
　　On dat mighty reck'nin' day,
When we'se reco'nised ez citiz'—
　　Huh uh! Chillun, let us pray!

Misapprehension

Out of my heart, one day, I wrote a song,
　　With my heart's blood imbued,
Instinct with passion, tremulously strong,
　　With grief subdued;
　　Breathing a fortitude
　　　Pain-bought.
And one who claimed much love for what I wrought,
　　Read and considered it,
　　And spoke:
"Ay, brother,—'t is well writ,
　　But where's the joke?"

Harriet Beecher Stowe

She told the story, and the whole world wept
  At wrongs and cruelties it had not known
  But for this fearless woman's voice alone.
  She spoke to consciences that long had slept:
Her message, Freedom's clear reveille, swept
  From heedless hovel to complacent throne.
  Command and prophecy were in the tone
  And from its sheath the sword of justice leapt.
Around two peoples swelled a fiery wave,
  But both came forth transfigured from the flame.
Blest be the hand that dared be strong to save,
  And blest be she who in our weakness came—
Prophet and priestess! At one stroke she gave
  A race to freedom and herself to fame.

Soliloquy of a Turkey

Dey's a so't o' threatenin' feelin' in de blowin' of de
      breeze,
  An' I's feelin' kin' o' squeamish in de night;
I's a-walkin' 'roun' a-lookin' at de diffunt style o' trees,
  An' a-measurin' dey thickness an' dey height.
Fu' dey's somep'n mighty 'spicious in de looks de da'kies
      give,
  Ez dey pass me an' my fambly in de groun',
So it 'curs to me dat lakly, ef I caihs to try an' live,
  It concehns me fu' to 'mence to look erroun'.

Dey's a cu'ious kin' o' shivah runnin' up an' down my
      back,
  An' I feel my feddahs rufflin' all de day,
An' my laigs commence to trimble evah blessid step I
      mek;
  W'en I sees a ax, I tu'ns my head away.
Folks is go'gin' me wid goodies, an' dey's treatin' me wid
      caih,

An' I's fat in spite of all dat I kin do.
I's mistrus'ful of de kin'ness dat's erroun' me evahwhaih,
    Fu' it's jes' too good, an' frequent, to be true.

Snow's a-fallin' on de medders, all erroun' me now is
    white,
    But I's still kep' on a-roostin' on de fence;
Isham comes an' feels my breas'-bone, an' he hefted me
    las' night,
    An' he's gone erroun' a-grinnin' evah sence.
'T ain't de snow dat meks me shivah; 't ain't de col' dat
    meks me shake;
    'T ain't de wintah-time itse'f dat's 'fectin' me;
But I t'ink de time is comin', an' I'd bettah mek a break,
    Fu' to set wid Mistah Possum in his tree.

W'en you hyeah de da'kies singin', an' de quahtahs all
    is gay,
    'T ain't de time fu' birds lak me to be 'erroun';
W'en de hick'ry chips is flyin', an' de log's been ca'ied
    erway,
    Den hit's dang'ous to be roostin' nigh de groun'.

Grin on, Isham! Sing on, da'kies! But I flop my wings
    an' go
    Fu' de sheltah of de ve'y highest tree,
Fu' dey's too much close ertention—an' dey's too much
    fallin' snow—
    An' it's too nigh Chris'mus mo'nin' now fu' me.

When Dey 'Listed Colored Soldiers

Dey was talkin' in de cabin, dey was talkin' in de hall;
But I listened kin' o' keerless, not a-t'inkin' 'bout it all;
An' on Sunday, too, I noticed, dey was whisp'rin' mighty
    much,
Stan'in' all erroun' de roadside w'en dey let us out o'
    chu'ch.

But I did n't t'ink erbout it 'twell de middle of de week,
An' my 'Lias come to see me, an' somehow he could n't
  speak.
Den I seed all in a minute whut he'd come to see me
  for;—
Dey had 'listed colo'ed sojers an' my 'Lias gwine to wah.

Oh, I hugged him, an' I kissed him, an' I baiged him
  not to go;
But he tol' me dat his conscience, hit was callin' to him
  so,
An' he could n't baih to lingah w'en he had a chanst
  to fight
For de freedom dey had gin him an' de glory of de right.
So he kissed me, an' he lef' me, w'en I'd p'omised to
  be true;
An' dey put a knapsack on him, an' a coat all colo'ed
  blue.
So I gin him pap's ol' Bible f'om de bottom of de
  draw',—
W'en dey 'listed colo'ed sojers an' my 'Lias went to wah.

But I t'ought of all de weary miles dat he would have
  to tramp,
An' I could n't be contented w'en dey tuk him to de
  camp.
W'y my hea't nigh broke wid grievin' 'twell I seed him
  on de street;
Den I felt lak I could go an' th'ow my body at his feet.
For his buttons was a-shinin', an' his face was shinin',
  too,
An' he looked so strong an' mighty in his coat o' sojer
  blue,
Dat I hollahed, "Step up, manny," dough my th'oat was
  so' an' raw,—
W'en dey 'listed colo'ed sojers an' my 'Lias went to wah.

Ol' Mis' cried w'en mastah lef' huh, young Miss mou'ned
  huh brothah Ned,
An' I did n't know dey feelin's is de ve'y wo'ds dey said

W'en I tol' 'em I was so'y. Dey had done gin up dey
all;
But dey only seemed mo' proudah dat dey men had
hyeahed de call.
Bofe my mastahs went in gray suits, an' I loved de Yan-
kee blue,
But I t'ought dat I could sorrer for de losin' of 'em too;
But I could n't, for I did n't know de ha'f o' whut I
saw,
'Twell dey 'listed colo'ed sojers an' my 'Lias went to wah.

Mastah Jack come home all sickly; he was broke for life,
dey said;
An' dey lef' my po' young mastah some'r's on de road-
side,—dead.
W'en de women cried an' mou'ned 'em, I could feel it
thoo an' thoo,
For I had a loved un fightin' in de way o' dangah, too.
Den dey tol' me dey had laid him some'r's way down
souf to res',
Wid de flag dat he had fit for shinin' daih acrost his
breas'.
Well, I cried, but den I reckon dat's whut Gawd had
called him for,
W'en dey 'listed colo'ed sojers an' my 'Lias went to wah.

To a Captious Critic

Dear critic, who my lightness so deplores,
Would I might study to be prince of bores,
Right wisely would I rule that dull estate—
But, sir, I may not, till you abdicate.

In the Morning

'Lias! 'Lias! Bless de Lawd!
Don' you know de day's erbroad?
Ef you don't git up, you scamp,
Dey'll be trouble in dis camp.
T'ink I gwine to let you sleep
W'ile I meks yo' boa'd an' keep?
Dat's a putty howdy-do—
Don' you hyeah me, 'Lias—you?

Bet ef I come crost dis flo'
You won' fin' no time to sno'.
Daylight all a-shinin' in
W'ile you sleep—w'y hit's a sin!
Ain't de can'le-light enough
To bu'n out widout a snuff,
But you go de mo'nin' thoo
Bu'nin' up de daylight too?

'Lias, don' you hyeah me call?
No use tu'nin' to'ds de wall:
I kin hyeah dat mattus squeak;
Don' you hyeah me w'en I speak?
Dis hyeah clock done struck off six—
Ca'line, bring me dem ah sticks!
Oh, you down, suh; huh, you down—
Look hyeah, don't you daih to frown.

Ma'ch yo'se'f an' wash yo' face,
Don' you splattah all de place;
I got somep'n else to do,
'Sides jes' cleanin' aftah you.
Tek dat comb an' fix yo' haid—
Looks jes' lak a feddah baid.
Look hyeah, boy, I let you see
You sha' n't roll yo' eyes at me.

Come hyeah; bring me dat ah strap!
Boy, I'll whup you 'twell you drap;
You done felt yo'se'f too strong,
An' you sholy got me wrong.
Set down at dat table thaih;
Jes' you whimpah ef you daih!
Evah mo'nin' on dis place,
Seem lak I mus' lose my grace.

Fol' yo' han's an' bow yo' haid—
Wait ontwell de blessin' 's said;
"Lawd, have mussy on ouah souls—"
(Don' you daih to tech dem rolls—)
"Bless de food we gwine to eat—"
(You set still—I *see* yo' feet;
You jes' try dat trick agin!)
"Gin us peace an' joy. Amen!"

The Poet

He sang of life, serenely sweet,
  With, now and then, a deeper note.
  From some high peak, nigh yet remote,
He voiced the world's absorbing beat.

He sang of love when earth was young,
  And Love, itself, was in his lays.
  But ah, the world, it turned to praise
A jingle in a broken tongue.

A Spiritual

De 'cession's stahted on de gospel way,
  De Capting is a-drawin' nigh:
Bettah stop a-foolin' an' a-try to pray;
  Lif' up yo' haid w'en de King go by!

Oh, sinnah mou'nin' in de dusty road,
  Hyeah's de minute fu' to dry yo' eye:
Dey's a moughty One a-comin' fu' to baih yo' load;
  Lif' up yo' haid w'en de King go by!

Oh, widder weepin' by yo' husban's grave,
  Hit's bettah fu' to sing den sigh:
Hyeah come de Mastah wid de powah to save;
  Lif' up yo' haid w'en de King go by!

Oh, orphans a-weepin' lak de widder do,
  An' I wish you'd tell me why:
De Mastah is a mammy an' a pappy too;
  Lif' up yo' haid w'en de King go by!

Oh, Moses sot de sarpint in de wildahness
  W'en de chillun had commenced to die:
Some 'efused to look, but hit cuohed de res';
  Lif' up yo' haid w'en de King go by!

Bow down, bow 'way down, Bow down,
But lif' up yo' haid w'en de King go by!

The Unsung Heroes

A song for the unsung heroes who rose in the country's
need,
When the life of the land was threatened by the slaver's
cruel greed,
For the men who came from the cornfield, who came
from the plough and the flail,
Who rallied round when they heard the sound of the
mighty man of the rail.

They laid them down in the valleys, they laid them down
in the wood,
And the world looked on at the work they did, and whis-
pered, "It is good."
They fought their way on the hillside, they fought their
way in the glen,
And God looked down on their sinews brown, and said,
"I have made them men."

They went to the blue lines gladly, and the blue lines
took them in,
And the men who saw their muskets' fire thought not
of their dusky skin.
The gray lines rose and melted beneath their scathing
showers,
And they said, " 'T is true, they have force to do, these
old slave boys of ours."

Ah, Wagner saw their glory, and Pillow knew their blood,
That poured on a nation's altar, a sacrificial flood.
Port Hudson heard their war-cry that smote its smoke-
filled air,
And the old free fires of their savage sires again were
kindled there.

They laid them down where the rivers, the greening val-
leys gem.
And the song of the thund'rous cannon was their sole
requiem,

And the great smoke wreath that mingled its hue with
    the dusky cloud,
Was the flag that furled o'er a saddened world, and the
    sheet that made their shroud.

Oh, Mighty God of the Battles Who held them in Thy
    hand,
Who gave them strength through the whole day's length,
    to fight for their native land,
They are lying dead on the hillsides, they are lying dead
    on the plain,
And we have not fire to smite the lyre and sing them
    one brief strain.

Give, Thou, some seer the power to sing them in their
    might,
The men who feared the master's whip, but did not fear
    the fight;
That he may tell of their virtues as minstrels did of old,
Till the pride of face and the hate of race grow obsolete
    and cold.

A song for the unsung heroes who stood the awful test,
When the humblest host that the land could boast went
    forth to meet the best;
A song for the unsung heroes who fell on the bloody
    sod,
Who fought their way from night to day and struggled
    up to God.

Philosophy

I been t'inkin' 'bout de preachah; whut he said de othah
    night,
    'Bout hit bein' people's dooty, fu' to keep dey faces
      bright;
How one ought to live so pleasant dat ouah tempah
    never riles,
    Meetin' evahbody roun' us wid ouah very nicest smiles.

Dat's all right, I ain't a-sputin' not a t'ing dat soun's lak
      fac',
    But you don't ketch folks a-grinnin' wid a misery in
      de back;
An' you don't fin' dem a-smilin' w'en dey's hongry ez kin
      be,
    Leastways, dat's how human natur' allus seems to 'pear
      to me.

We is mos' all putty likely fu' to have our little cares,
    An' I think we'se doin' fus' rate w'en we jes' go long
      and bears,
Widout breakin' up ouah faces in a sickly so't o' grin,
    W'en we knows dat in ouah innards we is p'intly mad
      ez sin.

Oh dey's times fu' bein' pleasant an' fu' goin' smilin'
      roun',
    'Cause I don't believe in people allus totin' roun' a
      frown,
But it's easy 'nough to titter w'en de stew is smokin' hot,
    But hit's mighty ha'd to giggle w'en dey's nuffin in de
      pot.

Compensation

Because I had loved so deeply,
    Because I had loved so long,
God in His great compassion
    Gave me the gift of song.

Because I have loved so vainly,
    And sung with such faltering breath,
The Master in infinite mercy
    Offers the boon of Death.

Harlem Renaissance

Esthete In Harlem

Strange,
That in this nigger place
I should meet life face to face;
When, for years, I had been seeking
Life in places gentler-speaking,
Until I came to this vile street
And found Life stepping on my feet!

LANGSTON HUGHES

CLAUDE McKAY (1890–1948)

The Harlem Dancer

Applauding youths laughed with young prostitutes
And watched her perfect, half-clothed body sway;
Her voice was like the sound of blended flutes
Blown by black players upon a picnic day.
She sang and danced on gracefully and calm,
The light gauze hanging loose about her form;
To me she seemed a proudly-swaying palm
Grown lovelier for passing through a storm.
Upon her swarthy neck black shiny curls
Luxuriant fell; and tossing coins in praise,
The wine-flushed, bold-eyed boys, and even the girls,
Devoured her shape with eager, passionate gaze;
But looking at her falsely-smiling face,
I knew her self was not in that strange place.

Spring in New Hampshire

(To J. L. J. F. E.)

Too green the springing April grass,
    Too blue the silver-speckled sky,
For me to linger here, alas,
    While happy winds go laughing by,
Wasting the golden hours indoors,
Washing windows and scrubbing floors.

Too wonderful the April night,
    Too faintly sweet the first May flowers,
The stars too gloriously bright,
    For me to spend the evening hours,

When fields are fresh and streams are leaping,
Wearied, exhausted, dully sleeping.

The Tired Worker

O whisper, O my soul! The afternoon
Is waning into evening, whisper soft!
Peace, O my rebel heart! for soon the moon
From out its misty veil will swing aloft!
Be patient, weary body, soon the night
Will wrap thee gently in her sable sheet,
And with a leaden sigh thou wilt invite
To rest thy tired hands and aching feet.
The wretched day was theirs, the night is mine;
Come tender sleep, and fold me to thy breast.
But what steals out the gray clouds red like wine?
Oh dawn! O dreaded dawn! O let me rest.
Weary my veins, my brain, my life! Have pity!
No! Once again the harsh, the ugly city.

To O.E.A.

Your voice is the color of a robin's breast,
    And there's a sweet sob in it like rain—still rain in
        the night.
Among the leaves of the trumpet-tree, close to his nest,
    The pea-dove sings, and each note thrills me with
        strange delight
Like the words, wet with music, that well from your
        trembling throat.
    I'm afraid of your eyes, they're so bold,
    Searching me through, reading my thoughts, shining
        like gold.
But sometimes they are gentle and soft like the dew on
        the lips of the eucharis

Before the sun comes warm with his lover's kiss.
You are sea-foam, pure with the star's loveliness,
Not mortal, a flower, a fairy, too fair for the beauty-shorn
earth.
All wonderful things, all beautiful things, gave of their
wealth to your birth.
Oh I love you so much, not recking of passion, that I
feel it is wrong!
But men will love you, flower, fairy, non-mortal
spirit burdened with flesh,
Forever, life-long.

The White City

I will not toy with it nor bend an inch.
Deep in the secret chambers of my heart
I muse my life-long hate, and without flinch
I bear it nobly as I live my part.
My being would be a skeleton, a shell,
If this dark Passion that fills my every mood,
And makes my heaven in the white world's hell,
Did not forever feed me vital blood.
I see the mighty city through a mist—
The strident trains that speed the goaded mass,
The poles and spires and towers vapor-kissed,
The fortressed port through which the great ships pass,
The tides, the wharves, the dens I contemplate,
Are sweet like wanton loves because I hate.

Enslaved

Oh when I think of my long-suffering race,
For weary centuries, despised, oppressed
Enslaved and lynched, denied a human place
In the great life line of the Christian West;
And in the Black Land disinherited,
Robbed in the ancient country of its birth,
My hearts grows sick with hate, becomes as lead,
For this my race that has no home on earth.
Then from the dark depth of my soul I cry
To the avenging angel to consume
The white man's world of wonders utterly:
Let it be swallowed up in earth's vast womb,
Or upward roll as sacrificial smoke
To liberate my people from its yoke!

Tiger

The white man is a tiger at my throat,
Drinking my blood as my life ebbs away,
And muttering that his terrible striped coat
Is Freedom's and portends the Light of Day.
Oh white man, you may suck up all my blood
And throw my carcass into potter's field,
But never will I say with you that mud
Is bread for Negroes! Never will I yield.

Europe and Africa and Asia wait
The touted New Deal of the New World's hand!
New systems will be built on race and hate,
The Eagle and the Dollar will command.
Oh Lord! My body, and my heart too, break—
The tiger in his strength his thirst must slake!

If We Must Die

If we must die, let it not be like hogs
Hunted and penned in an inglorious spot,
While round us bark the mad and hungry dogs,
Making their mock at our accursed lot.
If we must die, O let us nobly die,
So that our precious blood may not be shed
In vain; then even the monsters we defy
Shall be constrained to honor us though dead!
O kinsmen! we must meet the common foe!
Though far outnumbered let us show us brave,
And for their thousand blows deal one deathblow!
What though before us lies the open grave?
Like men we'll face the murderous, cowardly pack,
Pressed to the wall, dying, but fighting back!

The Negro's Tragedy

It is the Negro's tragedy I feel
Which binds me like a heavy iron chain,
It is the Negro's wounds I want to heal
Because I know the keenness of his pain.
Only a thorn-crowned Negro and no white
Can penetrate into the Negro's ken,
Or feel the thickness of the shroud of night
Which hides and buries him from other men.

So what I write is urged out of my blood.
There is no white man who could write my book,
Though many think their story should be told
Of what the Negro people ought to brook.
Our statesmen roam the world to set things right.
This Negro laughs and prays to God for Light!

Truth

Lord, shall I find it in Thy Holy Church,
Or must I give it up as something dead,
Forever lost, no matter where I search,
Like dinosaurs within their ancient bed?
I found it not in years of Unbelief,
In science stirring life like budding trees,
In Revolution like a dazzling thief—
Oh, shall I find it on my bended knees?

But what is Truth? So Pilate asked Thee, Lord,
So long ago when Thou wert manifest,
As the Eternal and Incarnate Word,
Chosen of God and by Him singly blest:
In this vast world of lies and hate and greed,
Upon my knees, Oh Lord, for Truth I plead.

The Pagan Isms

Around me roar and crash the pagan isms
To which most of my life was consecrate,
Betrayed by evil men and torn by schisms
For they were built on nothing more than hate!
I cannot live my life without the faith
Where new sensations like a fawn will leap,
But old enthusiasms like a wraith,
Haunt me awake and haunt me when I sleep.

And so to God I go to make my peace,
Where black nor white can follow to betray.
My pent-up heart to Him I will release
And surely He will show the perfect way
Of life. For He will lead me and no man
Can violate or circumvent His plan.

I Know My Soul

I plucked my soul out of its secret place,
And held it to the mirror of my eye,
To see it like a star against the sky,
A twitching body quivering in space,
A spark of passion shining on my face.
And I explored it to determine why
This awful key to my infinity
Conspires to rob me of sweet joy and grace.
And if the sign may not be fully read,
If I can comprehend but not control,
I need not gloom my days with futile dread,
Because I see a part and not the whole.
Contemplating the strange, I'm comforted
By this narcotic thought: I know my soul.

JEAN TOOMER (1894–1967)

Karintha

Her skin is like dusk on the eastern horizon,
O cant you see it, O cant you see it,
Her skin is like dusk on the eastern horizon
. . . When the sun goes down.

Men had always wanted her, this Karintha, even as a
child, Karintha carrying beauty, perfect as dusk when
the sun goes down. Old men rode her hobby-horse upon
their knees. Young men danced with her at frolics when
they should have been dancing with their grown-up
girls. God grant us youth, secretly prayed the old men.
The young fellows counted the time to pass before she
would be old enough to mate with them. This interest of
the male, who wishes to ripen a growing thing too soon,
could mean no good to her.

Karintha, at twelve, was a wild flash that told the
other folks just what it was to live. At sunset, when there
was no wind, and the pinesmoke from over by the saw-
mill hugged the earth, and you couldnt see more than
a few feet in front, her sudden darting past you was a
bit of vivid color, like a black bird that flashes in light.
With the other children one could hear, some distance
off, their feet flopping in the two-inch dust. Karintha's
running was a whir. It had the sound of the red dust
that sometimes makes a spiral in the road. At dusk,
during the hush just after the sawmill had closed down,
and before any of the women had started their supper-
getting-ready songs, her voice, high-pitched, shrill, would
put one's ears to itching. But no one ever thought to
make her stop because of it. She stoned the cows, and
beat her dog, and fought the other children . . . Even
the preacher, who caught her at mischief, told himself

that she was as innocently lovely as a November cotton flower. Already, rumors were out about her. Homes in Georgia are most often built on the two-room plan. In one, you cook and eat, in the other you sleep, and there love goes on. Karintha had seen or heard, perhaps she had felt her parents loving. One could but imitate one's parents, for to follow them was the way of God. She played "home" with a small boy who was not afraid to do her bidding. That started the whole thing. Old men could no longer ride her hobby-horse upon their knees. But young men counted faster.

> Her skin is like dusk,
> O cant you see it,
> Her skin is like dusk,
> When the sun goes down.

Karintha is a woman. She who carries beauty, perfect as dusk when the sun goes down. She has been married many times. Old men remind her that a few years back they rode her hobby-horse upon their knees. Karintha smiles, and indulges them when she is in the mood for it. She has contempt for them. Karintha is a woman. Young men run stills to make her money. Young men go to the big cities and run on the road. Young men go away to college. They all want to bring her money. These are the young men who thought that all they had to do was to count time. But Karintha is a woman, and she has had a child. A child fell out of her womb onto a bed of pine-needles in the forest. Pine-needles are smooth and sweet. They are elastic to the feet of rabbits . . . A sawmill was nearby. Its pyramidal sawdust pile smouldered. It is a year before one completely burns. Meanwhile, the smoke curls up and hangs in odd wraiths about the trees, curls up, and spreads itself out over the valley . . . Weeks after Karintha returned home the smoke was so heavy you tasted it in water. Some one made a song:

> Smoke is on the hills. Rise up.
> Smoke is on the hills, O rise
> And take my soul to Jesus.

Karintha is a woman. Men do not know that the soul of her was a growing thing ripened too soon. They will bring their money; they will die not having found it out ... Karintha at twenty, carrying beauty, perfect as dusk when the sun goes down. Karintha ...

> Her skin is like dusk on the eastern horizon,
> O cant you see it, O cant you see it,
> Her skin is like dusk on the eastern horizon
> ... When the sun goes down.

> Goes down ...

Reapers

Black reapers with the sound of steel on stones
Are sharpening scythes. I see them place the hones
In their hip-pockets as a thing that's done,
And start their silent swinging, one by one.
Black horses drive a mower through the weeds,
And there, a field rat, startled, squealing bleeds,
His belly close to ground. I see the blade,
Blood-stained, continue cutting weeds and shade.

Cotton Song

> Come, brother, come. Lets lift it;
> Come now, hewit! roll away!
> Shackles fall upon the Judgment Day
> But lets not wait for it.

> God's body's got a soul,
> Bodies like to roll the soul,
> Cant blame God if we dont roll,
> Come, brother, roll, roll!

Cotton bales are the fleecy way,
Weary sinner's bare feet trod,
Softly, softly to the throne of God,
"We aint agwine t wait until th Judgment Day!

Nassur; nassur,
Hump.
Eoho, eoho, roll away!
We aint agwine t wait until th Judgment Day!"

God's body's got a soul,
Bodies like to roll the soul,
Cant blame God if we dont roll,
Come, brother, roll, roll!

Georgia Dusk

The sky, lazily disdaining to pursue
    The setting sun, too indolent to hold
    A lengthened tournament for flashing gold,
Passively darkens for night's barbecue,

A feast of moon and men and barking hounds,
    An orgy for some genius of the South
    With blood-hot eyes and cane-lipped scented mouth,
Surprised in making folk-songs from soul sounds.

The sawmill blows its whistle, buzz-saws stop,
    And silence breaks the bud of knoll and hill,
    Soft settling pollen where plowed lands fulfill
Their early promise of a bumper crop.

Smoke from the pyramidal sawdust pile
    Curls up, blue ghosts of trees, tarrying low
    Where only chips and stumps are left to show
The solid proof of former domicile.

Meanwhile, the men, with vestiges of pomp,
    Race memories of king and caravan,
    High-priests, an ostrich, and a juju-man,
Go singing through the footpaths of the swamp.

Their voices rise . . the pine trees are guitars,
    Strumming, pine-needles fall like sheets of rain . .
    Their voices rise . . the chorus of the cane
Is caroling a vesper to the stars. .

O singers, resinous and soft your songs
    Above the sacred whisper of the pines,
    Give virgin lips to cornfield concubines,
Bring dreams of Christ to dusky cane-lipped throngs.

Evening Song

Full moon rising on the waters of my heart,
Lakes and moon and fires,
Cloine tires,
Holding her lips apart.

Promises of slumber leaving shore to charm the moon,
Miracle made vesper-keeps,
Cloine sleeps,
And I'll be sleeping soon.

Cloine, curled like the sleepy waters where the moon-
    waves start,
Radiant, resplendently she gleams,
Cloine dreams,
Lips pressed against my heart.

FRANK HORNE (1899–   )

Letters Found Near a Suicide:

To Mother

I came
in the blinding sweep
of ecstatic pain,
I go
in the throbbing pulse
of aching space—
in the aeons between
I piled upon you
pain on pain
ache on ache
and yet as I go
I shall know
that you will grieve
and want me back . . .

To 'Chick'

Oh Achilles of the moleskins
and the gridiron
do not wonder
nor doubt that this is I
that lies so calmly here—
this is the same exultant beast
that so joyously
ran the ball with you
in those far-flung days of abandon.
You remember how recklessly
we revelled in the heat and the dust
and the swirl of conflict?
You remember they called us
The Terrible Two?

And you remember
after we had battered our heads
and our bodies
against the stonewall of their defense,
you remember the signal I would call
and how you would look at me
in faith and admiration
and say 'Let's go' . . .
how the lines would clash
and strain,
and how I would slip through
fighting and squirming
over the line
to victory.

You remember, Chick?
When you gaze at me here
let that same light
of faith and admiration
shine in your eyes
for I have battered the stark stonewall
before me . . .
I have kept faith with you
and now
I have called my signal,
found my opening
and slipped through
fighting and squirming
over the line
to victory . . .

To You

All my life
they have told me
that You
would save my soul
that only
by kneeling in Your house
and eating of Your body

and drinking of Your blood
could I be born again . . .
And yet
one night
in the tall black shadow
of a windy pine
I offered up
the Sacrifice of Body
upon the altar
of her breast . . .
You
who were conceived
without ecstacy
or pain
can You understand
that I knelt last night
in Your house
and ate of Your body
and drank of Your blood
. . . and thought only of her?

To James

Do you remember
how you won
that last race . . . ?
how you flung your body
at the start . . .
how your spikes
ripped the cinders
in the stretch . . .
how you catapulted
through the tape . . .
do you remember . . . ?
Don't you think
I lurched with you
out of those starting holes . . . ?
Don't you think
my sinews tightened
at those first

few strides . . .
and when you flew into the stretch
was not all my thrill
of a thousand races
in your blood . . . ?
At your final drive
through the finish line
did not my shout
tell of the
triumphant ecstacy
of victory . . . ?
Live
as I have taught you
to run, Boy—
it's a short dash.
Dig your starting holes
deep and firm
lurch out of them
into the straightaway
with all the power
that is in you
look straight ahead
to the finish line
think only of the goal
run straight
run high
run hard
save nothing
and finish
with an ecstatic burst
that carries you
hurtling
through the tape
to victory . . .

Walk

I am trying
to learn to walk again . . .
all tensed and trembling
I try so hard, so hard . . .

Not like the headlong patter
of new and anxious feet
or the vigorous flailing of the water
by young swimmers
beating
a new element
into submission . . .
It is more like
a timorous Lazarus
commanded
to take up the bed
on which he died . . .

I know I will walk again
into your healing
outstretched arms
in answer
to your tender command . . .

I have been lost
and fallen
in the dark underbrush
but I will arise
and walk
and find the path
at your soft command.

'Mamma!'

This will really try you

. . . when I scampered
from pillar to post
on gay wandering
little feet
you watched with proud eyes
and a little hurt
that I was toddling
without clutching your skirt . . .
and when little Jack
stumbled
and fell down
bumping his little crown,
with swift soft embrace
and warm hungering lips
you kissed away
the pain
and the sudden fear
and the easy tears
and I scampered off
revived and whole again . . .

This faltering leg
and this unconscious arm
would really try you—

but I can already feel the touch
of your hand
groping
out of shrouded mist
and the soft caress of your lips
awakening new life . . .

I scampered
and fell . . .
—Mamma! . . . Mamma! . . .

Patience

Patience . . . patience
they all say . . .
but will patience
climb up a stair
or pick up a spoon
or chant a litany?
. . . those hollows
worn in a cathedral step
by the long slow prayers
of countless worshippers kneeling . . .

But I do not have a hundred years
nor forty
nor ten—
O You they call Eternal
to whom a thousand years
are but the wink of a languid eye—
help me to crowd
years of patient trial
and error
into the few flying days
I have . . .
Lend me but a jot
of Your aeon-packed
eternity
compress its infinite patience
into hours
and minutes
if it be Thy will
and the paean of my earthly gratitude
will reach up
and shake the very pillars
of the everlasting heavens . . .

LANGSTON HUGHES (1902–67)

The Negro Speaks of Rivers

(To W.E.B. DuBois)

I've known rivers:
I've known rivers ancient as the world and older than the
    flow of human blood in human veins.

My soul has grown deep like the rivers.

I bathed in the Euphrates when dawns were young.
I built my hut near the Congo and it lulled me to sleep.
I looked upon the Nile and raised the pyramids above it.
I heard the singing of the Mississippi when Abe Lincoln
    went down to New Orleans, and I've seen its muddy
    bosom turn all golden in the sunset.

I've known rivers:
Ancient, dusky rivers.

My soul has grown deep like the rivers.

Dinner Guest: Me

    I know I am
    The Negro Problem
    Being wined and dined,
    Answering the usual questions
    That come to white mind
    Which seeks demurely
    To probe in polite way
    The why and wherewithal

Of darkness U.S.A.—
Wondering how things got this way
In current democratic night,
Murmuring gently
Over *fraises du bois*,
"I'm so ashamed of being white."

The lobster is delicious,
The wine divine,
And center of attention
At the damask table, mine.
To be a Problem on
Park Avenue at eight
Is not so bad.
Solutions to the Problem,
Of course, wait.

Un-American Investigators

The committee's fat,
Smug, almost secure
Co-religionists
Shiver with delight
In warm manure
As those investigated—
Too brave to name a name—
Have pseudonyms revealed
In Gentile game
      Of who,
      Born Jew,
      Is who?
Is not your name Lipshitz?
      Yes.
*Did you not change it
For subversive purposes?*
      No.
For nefarious gain?
      Not so.

Are you sure?
The committee shivers
With delight in
Its manure.

Third Degree

Hit me! Jab me!
Make me say I did it.
Blood on my sport shirt
And my tan suede shoes.

Faces like jack-o'-lanterns
In gray slouch hats.

Slug me! Beat me!
Scream jumps out
Like blowtorch.
Three kicks between the legs
That kill the kids
I'd make tomorrow.

Bars and floor skyrocket
And burst like Roman candles.

When you throw
Cold water on me,
I'll sign the
Paper . . .

Who But the Lord?

I looked and I saw
That man they call the Law.
He was coming
Down the street at me!
I had visions in my head
Of being laid out cold and dead,
Or else murdered
By the third degree.

I said, O, Lord, if you can,
Save me from that man!
Don't let him make a pulp out of me!
But the Lord he was not quick.
The Law raised up his stick
And beat the living hell
Out of me!

Now I do not understand
Why God don't protect a man
From police brutality.
Being poor and black,
I've no weapon to strike back
So who but the Lord
Can protect me?

We'll see.

Ku Klux

They took me out
To some lonesome place.
They said, "Do you believe
In the great white race?"

I said, "Mister,
To tell you the truth,
I'd believe in anything
If you'd just turn me loose."

The white man said, "Boy,
Can it be
You're a-standin' there
A-sassin' me?"

They hit me in the head
And knocked me down.
And then they kicked me
On the ground.

A klansman said, "Nigger,
Look me in the face—
And tell me you believe in
The great white race."

Peace

We passed their graves:
The dead men there,
Winners or losers,
Did not care.

In the dark
They could not see
Who had gained
The victory.

Still Here

I been scarred and battered.
My hopes the wind done scattered.
      Snow has friz me,
      Sun has baked me,
Looks like between 'em they done
      Tried to make me
Stop laughin', stop lovin', stop livin'—
      But I don't care!
      I'm still here!

Cultural Exchange

In the Quarter of the Negroes
Where the doors are doors of paper
Dust of dingy atoms
Blows a scratchy sound.
Amorphous jack-o'-lanterns caper
And the wind won't wait for midnight
For fun to blow doors down.

By the river and the railroad
With fluid far-off going
Boundaries bind unbinding
A whirl of whistles blowing.
No trains or steamboats going—
Yet Leontyne's unpacking.

In the Quarter of the Negroes
Where the doorknob lets in Lieder
More than German ever bore,
Her yesterday past grandpa—
Not of her own doing—
In a pot of collard greens
Is gently stewing.

Pushcarts fold and unfold
In a supermarket sea.
And we better find out, mama,
Where is the colored laundromat
Since we moved up to Mount Vernon.

In the pot behind the paper doors
On the old iron stove what's cooking?
What's smelling, Leontyne?
Lieder, lovely Lieder
And a leaf of collard green.
Lovely Lieder, Leontyne.

You know, right at Christmas
They asked me if my blackness,
Would it rub off?
I said, *Ask your mama.*

Dreams and nightmares!
Nightmares, dreams, oh!
Dreaming that the Negroes
Of the South have taken over—
Voted all the Dixiecrats
Right out of power—
Comes the COLORED HOUR:
Martin Luther King is Governor of Georgia,
Dr. Rufus Clement his Chief Adviser,
A. Philip Randolph the High Grand Worthy.
In white pillared mansions
Sitting on their wide verandas,
Wealthy Negroes have white servants,
White sharecroppers work the black plantations,
And colored children have white mammies:
            Mammy Faubus
            Mammy Eastland
            Mammy Wallace
Dear, dear darling old white mammies—
Sometimes even buried with our family.
            Dear old
            Mammy Faubus!

Culture, they say, *is a two-way street:*
Hand me my mint julep, mammy.
          Hurry up!
          Make haste!

Junior Addict

The little boy
who sticks a needle in his arm
and seeks an out in other worldly dreams,
who seeks an out in eyes that droop
and ears that close to Harlem screams,
cannot know, of course,
(and has no way to understand)
a sunrise that he cannot see
beginning in some other land—
but destined sure to flood—and soon—
the very room in which he leaves
his needle and his spoon,
the very room in which today the air
is heavy with the drug
of his despair.

          (Yet little can
          tomorrow's sunshine give
          to one who will not live.)

Quick, sunrise, come—
Before the mushroom bomb
Pollutes his stinking air
With better death
Than is his living here,
With viler drugs
Than bring today's release
In poison from the fallout
Of our peace.

          *"It's easier to get dope
          than it is to get a job."*

Yes, easier to get dope
than to get a job—
daytime or nightime job,
teen-age, pre-draft,
pre-lifetime job.

Quick, sunrise, come!
Sunrise out of Africa,
Quick, come!
Sunrise, please come!
Come! Come!

Children's Rhymes

By what sends
the white kids
I ain't sent:
I know I can't
be President.

What don't bug
them white kids
sure bugs me:
We know everybody
ain't free.

Lies written down
for white folks
ain't for us a-tall:
Liberty And Justice—
Huh!—*For All?*

Words Like Freedom

There are words like *Freedom*
Sweet and wonderful to say.
On my heartstrings freedom sings
All day everyday.

There are words like *Liberty*
That almost make me cry.
If you had known what I know
You would know why.

Justice

That Justice is a blind goddess
Is a thing to which we black are wise:
Her bandage hides two festering sores
That once perhaps were eyes.

American Heartbreak

I am the American heartbreak—
The rock on which Freedom
Stumped its toe—
The great mistake
That Jamestown made
Long ago.

Frederick Douglass: 1817–1895

Douglass was someone who,
Had he walked with wary foot
And frightened tread,
From very indecision

Might be dead,
Might have lost his soul,
But instead decided to be bold
And capture every street
On which he set his feet,
To route each path
Toward freedom's goal,
To make each highway
Choose *his* compass' choice,
To all the world cried,
Hear my voice! . . .
Oh, to be a beast, a bird,
Anything but a slave! he said.

Who would be free
Themselves must strike
The first blow, he said.

He died in 1895.
He is not dead.

Where? When? Which?

When the cold comes
With a bitter fragrance
Like rusty iron and mint,
And the wind blows
Sharp as integration
With an edge like apartheid,
And it is winter,
And the cousins of the too-thin suits
Ride on bitless horses
Tethered by something worse than pride,
Which areaway, or bar,
Or station waiting room
Will not say,
Horse and horseman, outside!
With old and not too gentle
Apartheid?

Angola Question Mark

Don't know why I,
Black,
Must still stand
With my back
To the last frontier
Of fear
In my own land.

Don't know why I
Must turn into
A Mau Mau
And lift my hand
Against my fellow man
To live on my own land.

But it is so—
And being so
I know
For you and me
There's
Woe.

Question and Answer

Durban, Birmingham,
Cape Town, Atlanta,
Johannesburg, Watts,
The earth around
Struggling, fighting,
Dying—for what?

A world to gain.

Groping, hoping,
Waiting—for what?

A world to gain.

Dreams kicked asunder,
Why not go under?

There's a world to gain.

But suppose I don't want it,
Why take it?

To remake it.

The Backlash Blues

Mister Backlash, Mister Backlash,
Just who do you think I am?
Tell me, Mister Backlash,
Who do you think I am?
You raise my taxes, freeze my wages,
Send my son to Vietnam.

You give me second-class houses,
Give me second-class schools,
Second-class houses
And second-class schools.
You must think us colored folks
Are second-class fools.

When I try to find a job
To earn a little cash,
Try to find myself a job
To earn a little cash,
All you got to offer
Is a white backlash.

But the world is big,
The world is big and round,
Great big world, Mister Backlash,

Big and bright and round—
And it's full of folks like me who are
Black, Yellow, Beige, and Brown.

Mister Backlash, Mister Backlash,
What do you think I got to lose?
Tell me, Mister Backlash,
What you think I got to lose?
I'm gonna leave you, Mister Backlash,
Singing your mean old backlash blues.

You're the one,
Yes, you're the one
Will have the blues.

Warning

Negroes,
Sweet and docile,
Meek, humble, and kind:
Beware the day
They change their mind!

Wind
In the cotton fields,
Gentle breeze:
Beware the hour
It uproots trees!

ARNA BONTEMPS (1902–   )

God Give to Men

God give the yellow man
an easy breeze at blossom time.
Grant his eager, slanting eyes to cover
every land and dream
of afterwhile.

Give blue-eyed men their swivel chairs
to whirl in tall buildings.
Allow them many ships at sea,
and on land, soldiers
and policemen.

For black man, God,
no need to bother more
but only fill afresh his meed
of laughter,
his cup of tears.

God suffer little men
the taste of soul's desire.

Reconnaissance

After the cloud embankments,
the lamentation of wind
and the starry descent into time,
we came to the flashing waters and shaded our eyes
from the glare.

Alone with the shore and the harbor,
the stems of the cocoanut trees,

the fronds of silence and hushed music,
we cried for the new revelation
and waited for miracles to rise.

Where elements touch and merge,
where shadows swoon like outcasts on the sand
and the tried moment waits, its courage gone—
there were we

in latitudes where storms are born.

Nocturne of the Wharves

All night they whine upon their ropes and boom
against the dock with helpless prows:
these little ships that are too worn for sailing
front the wharf but do not rest at all.
Tugging at the dim gray wharf they think
no doubt of China and of bright Bombay,
and they remember islands of the East,
Formosa and the mountains of Japan.
They think of cities ruined by the sea
and they are restless, sleeping at the wharf.

Tugging at the dim gray wharf they think
no less of Africa. An east wind blows
and salt spray sweeps the unattended decks.
Shouts of dead men break upon the night.
The captain calls his crew and they respond—
the little ships are dreaming—land is near.
But mist comes up to dim the copper coast,
mist dissembles images of the trees.
The captain and his men alike are lost
and their shouts go down in the rising sound of waves.

Ah little ships, I know your weariness!
I know the sea-green shadows of your dream.
For I have loved the cities of the sea,

and desolations of the old days I
have loved: I was a wanderer like you
and I have broken down before the wind.

A Black Man Talks of Reaping

I have sown beside all waters in my day.
I planted deep, within my heart the fear
that wind or fowl would take the grain away.
I planted safe against this stark, lean year.

I scattered seed enough to plant the land
in rows from Canada to Mexico
but for my reaping only what the hand
can hold at once is all that I can show.

Yet what I sowed and what the orchard yields
my brother's sons are gathering stalk and root;
small wonder then my children glean in fields
they have not sown, and feed on bitter fruit.

COUNTEE CULLEN (1903–46)

Heritage

(For Harold Jackman)

What is Africa to me:
Copper sun or scarlet sea,
Jungle star or jungle track,
Strong bronzed men, or regal black
Women from whose loins I sprang
When the birds of Eden sang?
One three centuries removed
From the scenes his fathers loved,
Spicy grove, cinnamon tree,
What is Africa to me?

So I lie, who all day long
Want no sound except the song
Sung by wild barbaric birds
Goading massive jungle herds,
Juggernauts of flesh that pass
Trampling tall defiant grass
Where young forest lovers lie,
Plighting troth beneath the sky.
So I lie, who always hear,
Though I cram against my ear
Both my thumbs, and keep them there,
Great drums throbbing through the air.
So I lie, whose fount of pride,
Dear distress, and joy allied,
Is my somber flesh and skin,
With the dark blood dammed within
Like great pulsing tides of wine
That, I fear, must burst the fine
Channels of the chafing net
Where they surge and foam and fret.

Africa? A book one thumbs
Listlessly, till slumber comes.
Unremembered are her bats
Circling through the night, her cats
Crouching in the river reeds,
Stalking gentle flesh that feeds
By the river brink; no more
Does the bugle-throated roar
Cry that monarch claws have leapt
From the scabbards where they slept.
Silver snakes that once a year
Doff the lovely coats you wear,
Seek no covert in your fear
Lest a mortal eye should see;
What's your nakedness to me?
Here no leprous flowers rear
Fierce corollas in the air;
Here no bodies sleek and wet,
Dripping mingled rain and sweat,
Tread the savage measures of
Jungle boys and girls in love.
What is last year's snow to me,
Last year's anything? The tree
Budding yearly must forget
How its past arose or set—
Bough and blossom, flower, fruit,
Even what shy bird with mute
Wonder at her travail there,
Meekly labored in its hair.
One three centuries removed
From the scenes his father loved,
Spicy grove, cinnamon tree,
What is Africa to me?

So I lie, who find no peace
Night or day, no slight release
From the unremittant beat
Made by cruel padded feet
Walking through my body's street.
Up and down they go, and back,

Treading out a jungle track.
So I lie, who never quite
Safely sleep from rain at night—
I can never rest at all
When the rain begins to fall;
Like a soul gone mad with pain
I must match its weird refrain;
Ever must I twist and squirm,
Writhing like a baited worm,
While its primal measures drip
Through my body, crying, "Strip!
Doff this new exuberance.
Come and dance the Lover's Dance!"
In an old remembered way
Rain works on me night and day.

Quaint, outlandish heathen gods
Black men fashion out of rods,
Clay, and brittle bits of stone,
In a likeness like their own,
My conversion came high-priced;
I belong to Jesus Christ,
Preacher of humility;
Heathen gods are naught to me.

Father, Son, and Holy Ghost,
So I make an idle boast;
Jesus of the twice-turned cheek,
Lamb of God, although I speak
With my mouth thus, in my heart,
Do I play a double part.
Ever at Thy glowing altar
Must my heart grow sick and falter,
Wishing He I served were black,
Thinking then it would not lack
Precedent of pain to guide it,
Let who would or might deride it;
Surely then this flesh would know
Yours had borne a kindred woe.
Lord, I fashion dark gods, too,

Daring even to give You
Dark despairing features where,
Crowned with dark rebellious hair,
Patience wavers just so much as
Mortal grief compels, while touches
Quick and hot, of anger, rise
To smitten cheek and weary eyes.
Lord, forgive me if my need
Sometimes shapes a human creed.

All day long and all night through,
One thing only must I do:
Quench my pride and cool my blood,
Lest I perish in the flood.
Lest a hidden ember set
Timber that I thought was wet
Burning like the dryest flax,
Melting like the merest wax,
Lest the grave restore its dead.
Not yet has my heart or head
In the least way realized
They and I are civilized.

Incident

(For Eric Walrond)

Once riding in old Baltimore,
    Heart-filled, head-filled with glee,
I saw a Baltimorean
    Keep looking straight at me.

Now I was eight and very small,
    And he was no whit bigger,
And so I smiled, but he poked out
    His tongue, and called me, "Nigger."

I saw the whole of Baltimore
From May until December;
Of all the things that happened there
That's all that I remember.

Simon the Cyrenian Speaks

He never spoke a word to me,
And yet He called my name;
He never gave a sign to me,
And yet I knew and came.

At first I said, "I will not bear
His cross upon my back;
He only seeks to place it there
Because my skin is black."

But He was dying for a dream,
And He was very meek,
And in His eyes there shone a gleam
Men journey far to seek.

It was Himself my pity bought;
I did for Christ alone
What all of Rome could not have wrought
With bruise of lash or stone.

From the Dark Tower

(To Charles S. Johnson)

We shall not always plant while others reap
The golden increment of bursting fruit,
Not always countenance, abject and mute,
That lesser men should hold their brothers cheap;
Not everlastingly while others sleep
Shall we beguile their limbs with mellow flute,
Not always bend to some more subtle brute;
We were not made eternally to weep.

The night whose sable breast relieves the stark,
White stars is no less lovely being dark,
And there are buds that cannot bloom at all
In light, but crumple, piteous, and fall;
So in the dark we hide the heart that bleeds,
And wait, and tend our agonizing seeds.

Yet Do I Marvel

I doubt not God is good, well-meaning, kind,
And did He stoop to quibble could tell why
The little buried mole continues blind,
Why flesh that mirrors Him must some day die,
Make plain the reason tortured Tantalus
Is baited by the fickle fruit, declare
If merely brute caprice dooms Sisyphus
To struggle up a never-ending stair.
Inscrutable His ways are, and immune
To catechism by a mind too strewn
With petty cares to slightly understand
What awful brain compels His awful hand.
Yet do I marvel at this curious thing:
To make a poet black, and bid him sing!

To Certain Critics

Then call me traitor if you must,
Shout treason and default!
Say I betray a sacred trust
Aching beyond this vault.
I'll bear your censure as your praise,
For never shall the clan
Confine my singing to its ways
Beyond the ways of man.

No racial option narrows grief,
Pain is no patriot,
And sorrow plaits her dismal leaf
For all as lief as not.
With blind sheep groping every hill,
Searching an oriflamme,
How shall the shepherd heart then thrill
To only the darker lamb?

Post-Renaissance

"Summertime and the Living . . ."

Nobody planted roses, he recalls,
but sunflowers gangled there sometimes,
tough-stalked and bold
and like the vivid children there unplanned.
There circus-poster horses curveted
in trees of heaven
above the quarrels and shattered glass,
and he was bareback rider of them all.

No roses there in summer—
oh, never roses except when people died—
and no vacations for his elders,
so harshened after each unrelenting day
that they were shouting-angry.
But summer was, they said, the poor folks' time
of year. And he remembers
how they would sit on broken steps amid

The fevered tossings of the dusk, the dark,
wafting hearsay with funeral-parlor fans
or making evening solemn by
their quietness. Feels their Mosaic eyes
upon him, though the florist roses
that only sorrow could afford
long since have bidden them Godspeed.

Oh, summer summer summertime—

Then grim street preachers shook
their tambourines and Bibles in the face
of tolerant wickedness;
then Elks parades and big splendiferous
Jack Johnson in his diamond limousine
set the ghetto burgeoning
with fantasies
of Ethiopia spreading her gorgeous wings.

ROBERT HAYDEN

STERLING A. BROWN (1900–   )

Slim In Hell

I

Slim Greer went to heaven;
    St. Peter said, "Slim,
You been a right good boy."
    An' he winked at him.

        "You been a travelin' rascal
            In yo' day.
        You kin roam once mo';
            Den you come to stay.

"Put dese wings on yo' shoulders,
    An' save yo' feet."
Slim grin, and he speak up,
    "Thankye, Pete."

        Den Peter say, "Go
            To Hell an' see,
        All dat is doing, and
            Report to me.

"Be sure to remember
    How everything go."
Slim say, "I be seein' yuh
    On de late watch, bo."

        Slim got to cavortin'
            Swell as you choose,
        Like Lindy in de Spirit
            Of St. Louis Blues.

He flew an' he flew,
    Till at last he hit

A hangar wid de sign readin'
    DIS IS IT.

        Den he parked his wings,
            An' strolled aroun',
        Gittin' used to his feet
            On de solid ground.

II

Big bloodhound came aroarin'
    Like Niagry Falls,
Sicked on by white devils
    In overhalls.

Now Slim warn't scared,
    Cross my heart, it's a fac',
An de dog went on a bayin'
    Some po' devil's track.

        Den Slim saw a mansion
            An' walked right in;
        De Devil looked up
            Wid a sickly grin.

"Suttinly didn't look
    Fo' you, Mr. Greer,
How it happen you comes
    To visit here?"

        Slim say—"Oh, jes' thought
            I'd drop by a spell."
        "Feel at home, seh, an' here's
            De keys to hell."

Den he took Slim around
    An' showed him people
Rasin' hell as high as
    De First Church Steeple.

Lots of folks fightin'
   At de roulette wheel,
Like old Rampart Street,
   Or leastwise Beale.

Showed him bawdy houses
   An' cabarets,
Slim thought of New Orleans
   An' Memphis days.

      Each devil was busy
         Wid a devilish broad,
      An' Slim cried, "Lawdy,
         Lawd, Lawd, Lawd."

Took him in a room
   Where Slim see
De preacher wid a brownskin
   On each knee.

      Showed him giant stills,
         Going everywhere,
      Wid a passel of devils
         Stretched dead drunk there.

Den he took him to de furnace
   Dat some devils was firing,
Hot as hell, an' Slim start
   A mean presspirin'.

      White devils wid pitchforks
         Threw black devils on,
      Slim thought he'd better
         Be gittin' along.

An' he say—"Dis makes
   Me think of home—
Vicksburg, Little Rock, Jackson,
   Waco and Rome."

Den de devil gave Slim
De big Ha-Ha;
An' turned into a cracker,
Wid a sheriff's star.

Slim ran fo' his wings,
Lit out from de groun'
Hauled it back to St. Peter,
Safety boun'.

III

St. Peter said, "Well,
You got back quick.
How's de devil? An' what's
His latest trick?"

An' Slim say, "Peter,
I really cain't tell,
The place was Dixie
That I took for hell."

Then Peter say, "You must
Be crazy, I vow,
Where'n hell dja think Hell *was*,
Anyhow?

"Git on back to de yearth,
Cause I got de fear,
You'se a leetle too dumb,
Fo' to stay up here . . ."

Old Lem

I talked to old Lem
And old Lem said:
   "They weigh the cotton
They store the corn
   We only good enough
   To work the rows;
They run the commissary
They keep the books
   We gotta be grateful
   For being cheated;
Whippersnapper clerks
Call us out of our name
   We got to say mister
   To spindling boys
They make our figgers
Turn somersets
We buck in the middle
   Say, 'Thankyuh, sah.'
      They don't come by ones
      They don't come by twos
      But they come by tens.

"They got the judges
They got the lawyers
They got the jury-rolls
They got the law
      They don't come by ones
They got the sheriffs
They got the deputies
      They don't come by twos
They got the shotguns
They got the rope
   We git the justice
   In the end
      And they come by tens.

"Their fists stay closed
Their eyes look straight
   Our hands stay open
   Our eyes must fall
      They don't come by ones
They got the manhood
They got the courage
      They don't come by twos
   We got to slink around,
   Hangtailed hounds.
They burn us when we dogs
They burn us when we men
      They come by tens. . . .

"I had a buddy
Six foot of man
Muscled up perfect
Game to the heart
      They don't come by ones
Outworked and outfought
Any man or two men
      They don't come by twos
He spoke out of turn
At the commissary
They gave him a day
To git out the county.
He didn't take it.
He said 'Come and get me.'
They came and got him.
      And they came by tens.
He stayed in the county—
He lays there dead.

      They don't come by ones
      They don't come by twos
      But they come by tens."

Southern Road

Swing dat hammer—hunh—
Steady, bo.
Swing dat hammer—hunh—
Steady, bo;
Ain't no rush, bebby,
Long ways to go.

Burner tore his—hunh—
Black heart away;
Burner tore his—hunh—
Black heart away;
Got me life, bebby,
An' a day.

Gal's on Fifth Street—hunh—
Son done gone;
Gal's on Fifth Street—hunh—
Son done gone;
Wife's in de ward, bebby,
Babe's not bo'n.

My ole man died—hunh—
Cussin' me;
My ole man died—hunh—
Cussin' me;
Ole lady rocks, bebby,
Huh misery.

Doubleshackled—hunh—
Guard behin';
Doubleshackled—hunh—
Guard behin';
Ball an' chain, bebby,
On my min'.

White man tell me—hunh—
Damn yo' soul;
White man tells me—hunh—

Damn yo' soul;
Got no need, bebby,
To be tole.

Chain gang nevah—hunh—
Let me go;
Chain gang nevah—hunh—
Let me go;
Po' los' boy, bebby,
Evahmo' . . .

Long Gone

I laks yo' kin' of lovin'
  Ain't never caught you wrong
But it jes ain' nachal
  Fo' to stay here long;

It jes ain' nachal
  Fo' a railroad man
With a itch fo' travelin'
  He cain't understan'. . . .

I looks at de rails
  An' I looks at de ties
An' I hears an ole freight
  Puffin' up de rise,

An' at nights on my pallet
  When all is still
I listens fo' de empties
  Bumpin' up de hill;

When I oughta be quiet
  I is got a itch
Fo' to hear de whistle blow
  Fo' de crossin' or de switch,

An' I knows de time's a nearin'
   When I got to ride
Though it's homelike and happy
   At your side.

You is done all you could do
   To make me stay;
'Tain't no fault of yours I'se leavin'—
   I'se jes dataway.

I is got to see some people
   I ain' never seen,
Gotta highball thu some country
   Whah I never been. . . .

I don't know which way I'm travelin'—
   Far or near,
All I knows fo' certain is
   I cain't stay here.

Ain't no call at all, sweet woman,
   Fo' to carry on—
Jes my name and jes my habit
   To be Long Gone. . . .

Strong Men

> *The strong men keep coming on.*
> —SANDBURG.

They dragged you from homeland,
They chained you in coffles,
They huddled you spoon-fashion in filthy hatches,
They sold you to give a few gentlemen ease.

They broke you in like oxen,
They scourged you,
They branded you,

They made your women breeders,
They swelled your numbers with bastards....
They taught you the religion they disgraced.

You sang:
  Keep a-inchin' along
  Lak a po' inch worm....

You sang:
  Bye and bye
  I'm gonna lay down dis heaby load....

You sang:
  Walk togedder, chillen,
  Dontcha git weary....

    The strong men keep a-comin' on
    The strong men git stronger.

They point with pride to the roads you built for them,
They ride in comfort over the rails you laid for them.
They put hammers in your hands
And said—Drive so much before sundown.

You sang:
  Ain't no hammah
  In dis lan',
  Strikes lak mine, bebby,
  Strikes lak mine.

They cooped you in their kitchens,
They penned you in their factories,
They gave you the jobs that they were too good for,
They tried to guarantee happiness to themselves
By shunting dirt and misery to you.

You sang:
  Me an' muh baby gonna shine, shine
  Me an' muh baby gonna shine.
    The strong men keep a-comin' on
    The strong men git stronger....

They bought off some of your leaders
You stumbled, as blind men will. . . .
They coaxed you, unwontedly soft-voiced. . . .
You followed a way.
Then laughed as usual.
They heard the laugh and wondered;
Uncomfortable;
Unadmitting a deeper terror. . . .
>   The strong men keep a-comin' on
>   Gittin' stronger. . . .

What, from the slums
Where they have hemmed you,
What, from the tiny huts
They could not keep from you—
What reaches them
Making them ill at ease, fearful?
Today they shout prohibition at you
"Thou shalt not this"
"Thou shalt not that"
"Reserved for whites only"
You laugh.

One thing they cannot prohibit—
>   The strong men . . . coming on
>   The strong men gittin' stronger.
>   Strong men. . . .
>   Stronger. . . .

Crispus Attucks McCoy

I sing of a hero, unsung, unrecorded,
known by the name of Crispus Attucks McCoy.
Born, bred in Boston, stepson of Garvey,
cousin of Trotter, godson of DuBois.
No monastic hairshirt stung flesh more bitterly
than the white coat in which he was arrayed.
But what was his agony on entering the drawing room
to hear a white woman say slowly: 'one spade.'

He threw up his job, his scorn was sublime
and he left the bridge party simply aghast.
Lo, see him striding out of the front door
a free man again, his infamy past.
Down at the Common, the cradle of freedom,
another shock nearly carried him away.
Someone called out: 'Shine!' and he let loose a blue
   streak
and the poor little bootblack slunk frightened away.
In a bakery window he read with a glance
'Brown Bettys for sale,' and his molars gnashed.
Up came the kerbstone, back went his trusty arm,
swift was his gesture; the plate glass was smashed.
On the sub Crispus could have committed murder,
mayhem and cannibalism when he heard a maid
say to the cherub opposite to her:
'Come over here darling, here's a little shade.'
But down at the gardens he knew was his refuge,
recompense for insults, solace for grief.
A Negro battler, Slugging Joe Johnson,
was fighting an Irishman, Battling Dan O'Keefe.
The garden was crammed: Mickeys, Kikes, Bohans,
Polaks and Dagoes all over the place.
Crispus strode in regally, boldly,
the sole representative of his race.
The fight was even. When Joey hit Dan
the heart of Crispus shone with a steady glow;
when Dan hit Joey, Crispus groaned: 'Foul,
oh the dirty, lowdown so and so.'
In the tenth round Dan got to swinging,
Joey was dazed and clinched and held,
when suddenly right behind Crispus
'Kill the nigger,' somebody yelled.
Crispus got up in all of his fury,
lightning bolts zig-zagged out of his eyes.
With a voice like thunder he blurted his challenge:
'Will the bastard who said that please arise?'
Thirtyfive thousand Nordics and Alpines,
Hebrews and Gentiles as one man arose.

See how our hero, armed with his noble cause
onward with righteousness to battle goes.
They found an ankle in Dedham, a thighbone in Mal-
    den,
an elbow in Somerville, both nostrils in Lynn.
And on Boston Common lay one of his eyebrows,
the cap of his knee and a piece of his shin.
Peabody Museum has one of his eardrums,
his sound heart was found in Lexington.
But over the reaches from Cape Cod to 'Frisco
the soul of our hero goes marching on.

MELVIN B. TOLSON (1900–66)

A Legend of Versailles

Lloyd George and Woodrow Wilson and Clemenceau—
The Big Three: England, America, and France—
Met at Versailles. The Tiger ached to know
About the myth to end war's dominance.

"One moment, gentlemen," the Tiger said.
"Do you really want a lasting peace?" And then
Lloyd George assented with his shaggy head
And Woodrow Wilson, nodding, chafed his chin.

"The price of such a peace is great. We must give
Up secret cartels, spheres of power and trade;
Tear down our tariff walls; let lesser breeds live
As equals; scrap the empires we have made."

The gentlemen protested, "You go too far."
The Tiger shouted, "You don't mean peace, but war!"

The Birth of John Henry

The night John Henry is born an ax
    of lightning splits the sky,
and a hammer of thunder pounds the earth,
    and the eagles and panthers cry!

John Henry—he says to his Ma and Pa:
    "Get a gallon of barleycorn.
I want to start right, like a he-man child,
    the night that I am born!"

Says: "I want some ham hocks, ribs, and jowls,
    a pot of cabbage and greens;
some hoecakes, jam, and buttermilk,
    a platter of pork and beans!"

John Henry's Ma—she wrings her hands,
    and his Pa—he scratches his head.
John Henry—he curses in giraffe-tall words,
    flops over, and kicks down the bed.

He's burning mad, like a bear on fire—
    so he tears to the riverside.
As he stoops to drink, Old Man River gets scared
    and runs upstream to hide!

Some say he was born in Georgia—O Lord!
    Some say in Alabam.
But it's writ on the rock at the Big Bend Tunnel:
    "Lousyana was my home. So scram!"

Satchmo

King Oliver of New Orleans
has kicked the bucket, but he left behind
old Satchmo with his red-hot horn
to syncopate the heart and mind.
The honky-tonks in Storyville
have turned to ashes, have turned to dust,
but old Satchmo is still around
like Uncle Sam's IN GOD WE TRUST.

Where, oh, where is Bessie Smith
with her heart as big as the blues of truth?
Where, oh, where is Mister Jelly Roll
with his Cadillac and diamond tooth?
Where, oh, where is Papa Handy
with his blue notes a-dragging from bar to bar?

Where, oh, where is bulletproof Leadbelly
with his tall tales and 12-string guitar?

Old Hip Cats,
when you sang and played the blues
the night Satchmo was born,
did you know hypodermic needles in Rome
couldn't hoodoo him away from his horn?
Wyatt Earp's legend, John Henry's, too,
is a dare and a bet to old Satchmo
when his groovy blues put headlines in the news
from the Gold Coast to cold Moscow.

Old Satchmo's
gravelly voice and tapping foot and crazy notes
set my soul on fire.
If I climbed
the seventy-seven steps of the Seventh
Heaven, Satchmo's high C would carry me higher!
Are you hip to this, Harlem? Are you hip?
On Judgment Day, Gabriel will say
after he blows his horn:
"I'd be the greatest trumpeter in the Universe,
if old Satchmo had never been born!"

FRANK MARSHALL DAVIS (1905–   )

Robert Whitmore

Having attained success in business
possessing three cars
one wife and two mistresses
a home and furniture
talked of by the town
and thrice ruler of the local Elks
Robert Whitmore
died of apoplexy
when a stranger from Georgia
mistook him
for a former Macon waiter.

Arthur Ridgewood, M.D.

He debated whether
as a poet
to have dreams and beans
or as a physician
have a long car and caviar.
Dividing his time between both
he died from a nervous breakdown
caused by worry
from rejection slips
and final notices from the Finance company.

Giles Johnson, Ph.D.

Giles Johnson
had four college degrees
knew the whyfore of this
the wherefore of that
could orate in Latin
or cuss in Greek
and, having learned such things
he died of starvation
because he wouldn't teach
and he couldn't porter.

ROBERT HAYDEN (1913–   )

Middle Passage

I.

Jesús Estrella, Esperanza, Mercy:

Sails flashing to the wind like weapons,
sharks following the moans the fever and the dying;
horror the corposant and compass rose.

Middle Passage:
   voyage through death
         to life upon these shores.

"10 April 1800—
Blacks rebellious. Crew uneasy. Our linguist says
their moaning is a prayer for death,
ours and their own. Some try to starve themselves.
Lost three this morning leaped with crazy laughter
to the waiting sharks, sang as they went under."

Desire, Adventure, Tartar, Ann:

Standing to America, bringing home
black gold, black ivory, black seed.

   Deep in the festering hold thy father lies,
   of his bones New England pews are made,
   those are altar lights that were his eyes.

Jesus Saviour Pilot Me
Over Life's Tempestuous Sea

We pray that Thou wilt grant, O Lord,
safe passage to our vessels bringing
heathen souls unto Thy chastening.

Jesus Saviour

"8 bells, I cannot sleep, for I am sick
with fear, but writing eases fear a little
since still my eyes can see these words take shape
upon the page & so I write, as one
would turn to exorcism. 4 days scudding,
but now the sea is calm again. Misfortune
follows in our wake like sharks (our grinning
tutelary gods). Which one of us
has killed an albatross? A plague among
our blacks—Ophthalmia: blindness—& we
have jettisoned the blind to no avail.
It spreads, the terrifying sickness spreads.
Its claws have scratched sight from the Capt.'s eyes
& there is blindness in the fo'c'sle
& we must sail 3 weeks before we come
to port."

What port awaits us, Davy Jones'
or home? I've heard of slavers drifting, drifting,
playthings of wind and storm and chance, their
    crews
gone blind, the jungle hatred
crawling up on deck.

Thou Who Walked On Galilee

"Deponent further sayeth *The Bella J*
left the Guinea Coast
with cargo of five hundred blacks and odd
for the barracoons of Florida:

"That there was hardly room 'tween-decks for half
the sweltering cattle stowed spoon-fashion there;
that some went mad of thirst and tore their flesh
and sucked the blood:

"That Crew and Captain lusted with the comeliest
of the savage girls kept naked in the cabins;

that there was one they called The Guinea Rose
and they cast lots and fought to lie with her:

"That when the Bo's'n piped all hands, the flames
spreading from starboard already were beyond
control, the negroes howling and their chains
entangled with the flames:

"That the burning blacks could not be reached,
that the Crew abandoned ship,
leaving their shrieking negresses behind,
that the Captain perished drunken with the wenches:

"Further Deponent sayeth not."

Pilot Oh Pilot Me

II.

Aye, lad, and I have seen those factories,
Gambia, Rio Pongo, Calabar;
have watched the artful mongos baiting traps
of war wherein the victor and the vanquished

Were caught as prizes for our barracoons.
Have seen the nigger kings whose vanity
and greed turned wild black hides of Fellatah,
Mandingo, Ibo, Kru to gold for us.

And there was one—King Anthracite we named him—
fetish face beneath French parasols
of brass and orange velvet, impudent mouth
whose cups were carven skulls of enemies:

He'd honor us with drum and feast and conjo
and palm-oil-glistening wenches deft in love,
and for tin crowns that shone with paste,
red calico and German-silver trinkets

Would have the drums talk war and send
his warriors to burn the sleeping villages

and kill the sick and old and lead the young
in coffles to our factories.

Twenty years a trader, twenty years,
for there was wealth aplenty to be harvested
from those black fields, and I'd be trading still
but for the fevers melting down my bones.

III.

Shuttles in the rocking loom of history,
the dark ships move, the dark ships move,
their bright ironical names
like jests of kindness on a murderer's mouth;
plough through thrashing glister toward
fata morgana's lucent melting shore,
weave toward New World littorals that are
mirage and myth and actual shore.

Voyage through death,
                    voyage whose chartings are unlove.

A charnel stench, effluvium of living death
spreads outward from the hold,
where the living and the dead, the horribly dying,
lie interlocked, lie foul with blood and excrement.

> *Deep in the festering hold thy father lies,*
> *the corpse of mercy rots with him,*
> *rats eat love's rotten gelid eyes.*
>
> *But, oh, the living look at you*
> *with human eyes whose suffering accuses you,*
> *whose hatred reaches through the swill of dark*
> *to strike you like a leper's claw.*
>
> *You cannot stare that hatred down*
> *or chain the fear that stalks the watches*
> *and breathes on you its fetid scorching breath;*
> *cannot kill the deep immortal human wish,*
> *the timeless will.*

"But for the storm that flung up barriers
of wind and wave, *The Amistad*, señores,
would have reached the port of Principe in two,
three days at most; but for the storm we should
have been prepared for what befell.
Swift as the puma's leap it came. There was
that interval of moonless calm filled only
with the water's and the rigging's usual sounds,
then sudden movement, blows and snarling cries
and they had fallen on us with machete
and marlinspike. It was as though the very
air, the night itself were striking us.
Exhausted by the rigors of the storm,
we were no match for them. Our men went down
before the murderous Africans. Our loyal
Celestino ran from below with gun
and lantern and I saw, before the cane-
knife's wounding flash, Cinquez,
that surly brute who calls himself a prince,
directing, urging on the ghastly work.
He hacked the poor mulatto down, and then
he turned on me. The decks were slippery
when daylight finally came. It sickens me
to think of what I saw, of how these apes
threw overboard the butchered bodies of
our men, true Christians all, like so much jetsam.
Enough, enough. The rest is quickly told:
Cinquez was forced to spare the two of us
you see to steer the ship to Africa,
and we like phantoms doomed to rove the sea
voyaged east by day and west by night,
deceiving them, hoping for rescue,
prisoners on our own vessel, till
at length we drifted to the shores of this
your land, America, where we were freed
from our unspeakable misery. Now we
demand, good sirs, the extradition of
Cinquez and his accomplices to La
Havana. And it distresses us to know

there are so many here who seem inclined
to justify the mutiny of these blacks.
We find it paradoxical indeed
that you whose wealth, whose tree of liberty
are rooted in the labor of your slaves
should suffer the august John Quincy Adams
to speak with so much passion of the right
of chattel slaves to kill their lawful masters
and with his Roman rhetoric weave a hero's
garland for Cinquez. I tell you that
we are determined to return to Cuba
with our slaves and there see justice done. Cin-
     quez—
or let us say 'the Prince'—Cinquez shall die."

The deep immortal human wish,
the timeless will:

Cinquez its deathless primaveral image,
life that transfigures many lives.

Voyage through death
          to life upon these shores.

Runagate Runagate

I.

Runs falls rises stumbles on from darkness into darkness
and the darkness thicketed with shapes of terror
and the hunters pursuing and the hounds pursuing
and the night cold and the night long and the river
to cross and the jack-muh-lanterns beckoning beckoning
and blackness ahead and when shall I reach that some-
     where
morning and keep on going and never turn back and
     keep on going

           Runagate
                      Runagate
                                 Runagate

Many thousands rise and go
many thousands crossing over

                              O mythic North
                              O star-shaped yonder Bible city

Some go weeping and some rejoicing
some in coffins and some in carriages
some in silks and some in shackles

        Rise and go or fare you well

No more auction block for me
no more driver's lash for me

        If you see my Pompey, 30 yrs of age,
        new breeches, plain stockings, negro shoes;
        if you see my Anna, likely young mulatto
        branded E on the right cheek, R on the left,
        catch them if you can and notify subscriber.
        Catch them if you can, but it won't be easy.
        They'll dart underground when you try to catch
            them,
        plunge into quicksand, whirlpools, mazes,
        turn into scorpions when you try to catch them

And before I'll be a slave
I'll be buried in my grave

        North star and bonanza gold
        I'm bound for the freedom, freedom-bound
        and oh Susyanna don't you cry for me

            Runagate

                      Runagate

II.

Rises from their anguish and their power,

> Harriet Tubman,

> woman of earth, whipscarred,
> a summoning, a shining

> Mean to be free

And this was the way of it, brethren brethren,
way we journeyed from Can't to Can.
Moon so bright and no place to hide,
the cry up and the patterollers riding,
hound dogs belling in bladed air.
And fear starts a-murbling, Never make it,
we'll never make it. *Hush that now,*
and she's turned upon us, levelled pistol
glinting in the moonlight:
Dead folks can't jaybird-talk, she says:
you keep on going now or die, she says.

Wanted   Harriet Tubman   alias The General
alias Moses   Stealer of Slaves

In league with Garrison   Alcott   Emerson
Garrett   Douglass   Thoreau   John Brown

Armed and known to be Dangerous

Wanted   Reward   Dead or Alive

> Tell me, Ezekiel, oh tell me do you see
> mailed Jehovah coming to deliver me?

Hoot-owl calling in the ghosted air,
five times calling to the hants in the air.
Shadow of a face in the scary leaves,
shadow of a voice in the talking leaves:

Come ride-a my train

Oh that train, ghost-story train
through swamp and savanna movering movering,
over trestles of dew, through caves of the wish,
Midnight Special on a sabre track movering mover-
    ing,
first stop Mercy and the last Hallelujah.

Come ride-a my train

Mean mean mean to be free.

A Ballad of Remembrance

Quadroon mermaids, Afro angels, black saints
balanced upon the switchblades of that air
and sang. Tight streets unfolding to the eye
like fans of corrosion and elegiac lace
crackled with their singing: Shadow of time. Shadow of
    blood.

Shadow, echoed the Zulu king, dangling
from a cluster of balloons. Blood,
whined the gun-metal priestess, floating
over the courtyard where dead men diced.

What will you have? she inquired, the sallow vendeuse
of prepared tarnishes and jokes of nacre and ormolu,
what but those gleamings, oldrose graces,
manners like scented gloves? Contrived ghosts
rapped to metronome clack of lavalieres.

Contrived illuminations riding a threat
of river, masked Negroes wearing chameleon
satins gaudy now as a fortuneteller's
dream of disaster, lighted the crazy flopping
dance of love and hate among joys, rejections.

Accommodate, muttered the Zulu king,
toad on a throne of glaucous poison jewels.
Love, chimed the saints and the angels and the mer-
    maids.
Hate, shrieked the gun-metal priestess
from her spiked bellcollar curved like a fleur-de-lis:

As well have a talon as a finger, a muzzle as a mouth,
as well have a hollow as a heart. And she pinwheeled
away in coruscations of laughter, scattering
those others before her like foil stars.

But the dance continued—now among metaphorical
doors, coffee cups floating poised
hysterias, decors of illusion; now among
mazurka dolls offering death's-heads
of cocaine roses and real violets.

Then you arrived, meditative, ironic,
richly human; and your presence was shore where I
    rested
released from the hoodoo of that dance, where I spoke
    with my true voice again.

And therefore this is not only a ballad of remembrance
for the down-South arcane city with death
in its jaws like gold teeth and archaic cusswords;
not only a token for the troubled generous friends
held in the fists of that schizoid city like flowers,
but also, Mark Van Doren,
a poem of remembrance, a gift, a souvenir for you.

The Ballad of Nat Turner

Then fled, O brethren, the wicked juba
    and wandered wandered far
from curfew joys in the Dismal's night.
    Fool of St. Elmo's fire

In scary night I wandered, praying,
    Lord God my harshener,
speak to me now or let me die;
    speak, Lord, to this mourner.

And came at length to livid trees
    where Ibo warriors
hung shadowless, turning in wind
    the moaned like Africa,

Their belltongue bodies dead, their eyes
    alive with the anger deep
in my own heart. Is this the sign,
    the sign forepromised me?

The spirits vanished. Afraid and lonely
    I wandered on in blackness.
Speak to me now or let me die.
    Die, whispered the blackness.

And wild things gasped and scuffled in
    the night; seething shapes
of evil frolicked upon the air.
    I reeled with fear, I prayed.

Sudden brightness clove the preying
    darkness, brightness that was
itself a golden darkness, brightness
    so bright that it was darkness.

And there were angels, their faces hidden
    from me, angels at war
with one another, angels in dazzling
    combat. And oh the splendor,

The fearful splendor of that warring.
    Hide me, I cried to rock and bramble.
Hide me, the rock, the bramble cried. . . .
    How tell you of that holy battle?

The shock of wing on wing and sword
    on sword was the tumult of
a taken city burning. I cannot
    say how long they strove,

For the wheel in a turning wheel which is time
    in eternity had ceased
its whirling, and owl and moccasin,
    panther and nameless beast

And I were held like creatures fixed
    in flaming, in fiery amber.
But I saw I saw oh many of
    those mighty beings waver,

Waver and fall, go streaking down
    into swamp water, and the water
hissed and steamed and bubbled and locked
    shuddering shuddering over

The fallen and soon was motionless.
    Then that massive light
began a-folding slowly in
    upon itself, and I

Beheld the conqueror faces and, lo,
    they were like mine, I saw
they were like mine and in joy and terror
    wept, praising praising Jehovah.

Oh praised my honer, harshener
    till a sleep came over me,
a sleep heavy as death. And when
    I awoke at last free

And purified, I rose and prayed
    and returned after a time
to the blazing fields, to the humbleness.
    And bided my time.

Full Moon

No longer throne of a goddess to whom we pray,
no longer the bubble house of childhood's
tumbling Mother Goose man,

The emphatic moon ascends—
the brilliant challenger of rocket experts,
the white hope of communications men.

Some I love who are dead
were watchers of the moon and knew its lore;
planted seeds, trimmed their hair,

Pierced their ears for gold hoop earrings
as it waxed or waned.
It shines tonight upon their graves.

And burned in the garden of Gethsemane,
its light made holy by the dazzling tears
with which it mingled.

And spread its radiance on the exile's path
of Him who was The Glorious One,
its light made holy by His holiness.

Already a mooted goal and tomorrow perhaps
an arms base, a livid sector,
the full moon dominates the dark.

The Diver

Sank through easeful
azure. Flower
creatures flashed and
shimmered there—
lost images
fadingly remembered.
Swiftly descended
into canyon of cold
nightgreen emptiness.
Freefalling, weightless
as in dreams of
wingless flight,
plunged through infra-
space and came to
the dead ship,
carcass that swarmed with
voracious life.
Angelfish, their
lively blue and
yellow prised from
darkness by the
flashlight's beam,
thronged her portholes.
Moss of bryozoans
blurred, obscured her
metal. Snappers,
gold groupers explored her,
fearless of bubbling
manfish. I entered
the wreck, awed by her silence,
feeling more keenly
the iron cold.
With flashlight probing
fogs of water
saw the sad slow
dance of gilded
chairs, the ectoplasmic
swirl of garments,

drowned instruments
of buoyancy,
drunken shoes. Then
livid gesturings,
eldritch hide and
seek of laughing
faces. I yearned to
find those hidden
ones, to fling aside
the mask and call to them,
yield to rapturous
whisperings, have
done with self and
every dinning
vain complexity.
Yet in languid
frenzy strove, as
one freezing fights off
sleep desiring sleep;
strove against the
cancelling arms that
suddenly surrounded
me, fled the numbing
kisses that I craved.
Reflex of life-wish?
Respirator's brittle
belling? Swam from
the ship somehow;
somehow began the
measured rise.

The Wheel

Gentle and smiling as before,
he stroked the leopard purring by his chair
and whispered silkily to me.
And though I knew he lied,
lied with every flicker of
his jewelled hands,

I listened and believed,
persuaded as before
by what he seemed to say
yet did not say.
And when, face close to mine,
he murmured that equivocal command,

I went to do his bidding as before.
And so once more,
the useless errand bitterly accomplished,
I crouch in the foulness of a ditch;
like traitor, thief or murderer hide
and curse the moon and fear the rising of the sun.

In the Mourning Time

As the gook woman howls
for her boy in the smouldering,
as the expendable Clean-Cut Boys
From Decent American Homes
are slashing off enemy ears for keepsakes;

as the victories are tallied up
with flag-draped coffins, plastic bodybags,
what can my sorrow anger pity say
but this, this:

We must not be frightened nor cajoled
into accepting evil as deliverance from evil.
We must go on struggling to be human,
though monsters of abstraction
police and threaten us.

Reclaim now, now renew the vision of
a human world where godliness
is possible and man
is neither gook nigger honkey wop nor kike

but man

            permitted to be man.

DUDLEY RANDALL (1914–   )

Analysands

Sipping whiskey and gin,
they analyze their analysts and their treatment
in jargon like the debris in a magpie's gullet.
Each feeling, each phrase, each dream
is dissected with dialectic keener than a scalpel.
Like lactating women unbrassiering and comparing their
    breasts
or small boys measuring their penises,
they incise themselves,
draw out and display their entrails,
tear out their throbbing dripping hearts
and scrutinize each minute quivering,
till finally, full of whiskey and gin,
they drop asleep on sofa, chair or floor.

Primitives

Paintings with stiff
homuncules, flat in iron
draperies, with distorted
bodies against spaceless
landscapes.

Poems of old
poets in stiff
metres whose harsh
syllables
drag like
dogs with
crushed
backs.

We go back to
them, spurn difficult
grace and
symmetry,
paint tri-faced
monsters,
write lines that
do not sing, or
even croak, but that
bump,
jolt, and are hacked
off in the mid-
dle, as if by these dis-
tortions, this
magic, we can
exorcise
horror, which we
have seen and fear to
see again:

hate deified,
fears and
guilt conquering,
turning cities to
gas, powder and a
little rubble.

Hail, Dionysos

Hail, Dionysos,
god of frenzy and release, of trance and visions,
hail to the manifestations of your might,
thanks for admitting me to your ritual.

Inspirer of divine speech:
    da da da da da da da da da;
releaser of subterranean energies:
    a man lies snoring on the sofa;

giver of fierce grace:
> *a girl staggers among chairs, reels against the wall;*

endower with new sensations and powers:
> *a man vomits on the rug—an aromatic painting,*
> *and a girl, a lovely creature,*
> *wets her panties.*

Hail, Dionysos,
god of frenzy and release, of trance and visions.

I see them recede,
handsome men, beautiful women,
brains clever and bright, spirits gay and daring,
see eyes turn glassy, tongues grow thick,
limbs tremble and shake,
caught in your divine power,
carried away on the stream of your might,
Dionysos.

The Melting Pot

There is a magic melting pot
where any girl or man
can step in Czech or Greek or Scot,
step out American.

Johann and *Jan* and *Jean* and *Juan,*
Giovanni and *Ivan*
step in and then step out again
all freshly christened *John.*

Sam, watching, said, "Why, I was here
even before they came,"
and stepped in too, but was tossed out
before he passed the brim.

And every time Sam tried that pot
they threw him out again.

"Keep out. This is our private pot.
We don't want your black stain."

At last, thrown out a thousand times,
Sam said, "I don't give a damn.
Shove your old pot. You can like it or not,
but I'll be just what I am."

A Different Image

The age
requires this task:
create
a different image;
re-animate
the mask.

Shatter the icons of slavery and fear.
Replace
the leer
of the minstrel's burnt-cork face
with a proud, serene
and classic bronze of Benin.

Roses and Revolutions

Musing on roses and revolutions,
I saw night close down on the earth like a great dark
    wing,
and the lighted cities were like tapers in the night,
and I heard the lamentations of a million hearts
regretting life and crying for the grave,
and I saw the Negro lying in the swamp with his face
    blown off,
and in northern cities with his manhood maligned and
    felt the writhing

of his viscera like that of the hare hunted down or the
    bear at bay,
and I saw men working and taking no joy in their work
and embracing the hard-eyed whore with joyless excite-
    ment
and lying with wives and virgins in impotence.

And as I groped in darkness
and felt the pain of millions,
gradually, like day driving night across the continent,
I saw dawn upon them like the sun a vision
of a time when all men walk proudly through the earth
and the bombs and missiles lie at the bottom of the
    ocean
like the bones of dinosaurs buried under the shale of
    eras,
and men strive with each other not for power or the ac-
    cumulation of paper
but in joy create for others the house, the poem, the
    game of athletic beauty.

Then washed in the brightness of this vision,
I saw how in its radiance would grow and be nourished
    and suddenly
burst into terrible and splendid bloom
the blood-red flower of revolution

Ballad of Birmingham

"Mother dear, my I go downtown
instead of out to play,
and march the streets of Birmingham
in a freedom march today?"

"No, baby, no, you may not go,
for the dogs are fierce and wild,
and clubs and hoses, guns and jails
ain't good for a little child."

"But, mother, I won't be alone.
Other children will go with me,
and march the streets of Birmingham
to make our country free."

"No, baby, no, you may not go,
for I fear those guns will fire.
But you may go to church instead,
and sing in the children's choir."

She has combed and brushed her nightdark hair,
and bathed rose petal sweet,
and drawn white gloves on her small brown hands,
and white shoes on her feet.

The mother smiled to know her child
was in the sacred place,
but that smile was the last smile
to come upon her face.

For when she heard the explosion,
her eyes grew wet and wild.
She raced through the streets of Birmingham
calling for her child.

She clawed through bits of glass and brick,
then lifted out a shoe.
"O, here's the shoe my baby wore,
but, baby, where are you?"

The Idiot

"That cop was powerful mean.
First, he called me, 'Black boy.'
Then he punched me in the face
and drug me by the collar to a wall
and made me lean against it with my hands on it
while he searched me,

and all the time he searched me
he kicked me and cuffed me and cussed me.

"I was hot enough
to lay him out,
and woulda did it, only
I didn't want to hurt his feelings,
and lose the good will
of the good white folks downtown,
who hired him."

George

When I was a boy desiring the title of man
And toiling to earn it
In the inferno of the foundry knockout,
I watched and admired you working by my side,
As, goggled, with mask on your mouth and shoulders
   bright with sweat,
You mastered the monstrous, lumpish cylinder blocks,
And when they clotted the line and plunged to the floor
With force enough to tear your foot in two,
You calmly stepped aside.

One day when the line broke down and the blocks
   reared up
Groaning, grinding, and mounted like an ocean wave
And then rushed thundering down like an avalanche,
And we frantically dodged, then braced our heads to-
   gether
To form an arch to lift and stack them,
You gave me your highest accolade:
You said: "You not afraid of sweat. You strong as
   a mule."

Now, here, in the hospital,
In a ward where old men wait to die,
You sit, and watch time go by.

You cannot read the books I bring, not even
Those that are only picture books,
As you sit among the senile wrecks,
The psychopaths, the incontinent.

One day when you fell from your chair and stared at
    the air
With the look of fright which sight of death inspires,
I lifted you like a cylinder block, and said,
"Don't be afraid
Of a little fall, for you'll be here
A long time yet, because you're strong as a mule."

Souvenirs

my love has left me has gone from me
    and I with no keepsake nothing
    not a glove handkerchief lock of hair picture
    only in memory

the first night the magic snowfall
    the warm blue-walled room we looking out at the
        snow
    listening to music drinking the same cocktail
    she pressing my hand searching my eyes
    the first kiss my hands touching her
    she close to me answering my lips
    waking at morning eyes opening slowly

I approaching her house trembling
    kissing her entering the room
    waking all night writing a poem for her
    thinking of her planning her pleasure
    remembering her least liking and desire
    she cooking for me eating with me
    kissing me with little kisses over the face
    we telling our lives till morning

more to remember better to forget
   she denying me slashing my love
   all pain forgotten if only she comes back to me

The Profile on the Pillow

After our fierce loving
in the brief time we found to be together,
you lay in the half light
exhausted, rich,
with your face turned sideways on the pillow,
and I traced the exquisite
line of your profile, dark against the white,
delicate and lovely as a child's.

Perhaps
you will cease to love me,
or we may be consumed in the holocaust,
but I keep, against the ice and the fire,
the memory of your profile on the pillow.

Abu

Abu
's a stone black revolutionary.
Decided to blow up City Hall.
Put full page ad in New York Times
announcing
his inten/
        shun.
Says rightinfrontof
F. B. I. in fil/
         trators
he gon sassinate
rich white liberal
gave only *half*
a million

to N. A. A. C. P.
Says nothin' 'bout that Southern sheriff
killed three black prisoners
'cept, he admire him
for his sin/
        cerity.

Ancestors

Why are our ancestors
always kings and princes
and never the common people?

Was the Old Country a democracy
where every man was a king?
Or did the slave-catchers
steal only the aristocrats
and leave the fieldhands
laborers
street cleaners
garbage collectors
dish washers
cooks
and maids
behind?

My own ancestor
(research reveals)
was a swineherd
who tended the pigs
in the Royal Pigstye
and slept in the mud
among the hogs.

Yet I'm as proud of him
as of any king or prince
dreamed up in fantasies
of bygone glory.

MARGARET DANNER

Garnishing the Aviary

"are you beautiful still?"

Our moulting days are in their twilight stage.
These lengthy dreaded suns of draggling plumes.
These days of moods that swiftly alternate between

the former preen and a downcast rage
or crest-fallen lag, are fading out. The initial bloom;
exotic, dazzling in its indigo, tangerine

splendor; this rare, conflicting coat had to be shed.
Our drooping feathers turn all shades. We spew
this unamicable aviary, gag upon the worm, and fling

our loosening quills. We make a riotous spread
upon the dust and mire that beds us. We do not shoo
so quickly; but the shades of the pinfeathers resulting

from this chaotic push, though still exotic,
blend in more easily with those on the wings
of the birds surrounding them; garnishing
the aviary, burnishing this zoo.

The Convert

When in nineteen-thirty-seven, Etta Moten, sweetheart
of our Art Study group, kept her promise, as if clocked,
to honor my house at our first annual tea, my pride

tipped sky, but when she, Parisian-poised and as smart
as a chrome-toned page from Harper's Bazaar, gave my
    shocked
guests this hideous African nude, I could have cried.

And for many subsequent suns, we, who had placed
    apart
this hour to proclaim our plunge into modern art,
    mocked
her "Isn't he lovely?" whenever we eyed this thing,

for by every rule we'd learned, we'd been led to discern
this rankling figure as ugly. It hunched in a squat
as if someone with maliciously disfiguring intent

had flattened it with a press, bashing its head,
bloating its features, making huge bulging blots
of its lips and nose, and as my eyes in dread anticipa-
    tion

pulled downward, there was its navel, without a thread
of covering, ruptured, exposed, protruding from a pot
stomach as huge as a mother-to-be's, on short, bent legs,

extending as far on each side as swollen back limbs
of a turtle. I could look no farther and nearly dispensed
with being polite while pretending to welcome her gift.

But afterwards, to the turn of calendar pages, my eyes
    would skim
the figure, appraising this fantastic sight,
until, finally, I saw on its stern

ebony face, not a furniture polished, shellacked shine,
but a radiance, gleaming as though a small light
had flashed internally; and I could discern

through the sheen that the bulging eyes
were identical twins to the bulging nose.
The same symmetrical form was dispersed again

and again through all the bulges, the thighs
and the hands and the lips, in reverse, even the toes
of this fast turning beautiful form were a selfsame chain,

matching the navel. This little figure stretched high
in grace, in its with-the-grain form and from-within-glow,
in its curves in concord. I became a hurricane

of elation, a convert undaunted, who wanted to flaunt
her discovery, parade her fair-contoured find.

Art clubs, like leaves in autumn fall,
scrabble against concrete and scatter.
And Etta Moten, I read, is at tea with the Queen.

But I find myself still framing word structures
of how much these blazing forms ascending the cen-
    turies
in their muted sheens, matter to me.

This Is an African Worm

This is an African worm
but then a worm in any land
is still a worm.

It will not stride, run, stand up
before the butterflies, who
have passed their worm-like state.

It must keep low, not lift its head.
I've had the dread experience, I know.
A worm can do no thing but crawl.

Crawl, and wait.

The Painted Lady

The Painted Lady is a small African
butterfly, gayly toned orchid or peach
that seems as tremulous and delicately sheer

as the objects I treasure, yet, this cosmopolitan
can cross the sea at the icy time of the year
in the trail of the big boats, to France.

Mischance is as wide and somber grey as the lake here
in Chicago. Is there strength enough in my huge
peach paper rose, or lavender sea-laced fan?

And through the Caribbean Sea

We, like shades that were first conjured up
by an African witch-doctor's ire,
(indigo for the drum and the smoke of night,

tangerine for the dancing smudged fire)
have been forced to exist in a huge kaleidoscope world.
We've been shifting with time and sifting through space,

at each whimsical turn of the hands that have thrown
the kaleidoscope, until any pattern or place
or shade is our own.

The indigo sifted from its drum-like vein
toward the blue of the sky that the Goths attained.
The tangerine, became the orange of the tango, again

the red of the Susy Q. and each time the turning invaded
one pattern, a new one was formed
and in forming each pattern, we traded.

Until, who questions whether we'd be prone to yearn
for a Louis Quinze frame, a voodoo fire,
Rococo, Baroque, an African mask or a Gothic spire
or any style of any age or any place or name.

Goodbye David Tamunoemi West

When you were here in wonderful Detroit,
   the sheer amazing might of TAMUNOEMI
   became my delightful, inspiring game.

And when the mad stampede descended,
   your signature, arrows of the Masai,
   searched out and pierced intended wrong.
   Since then the very marrow of my bones
   made of TAMUNOEMI a song.

A song that placed me close to Africa, enhanced
   my heritage, and I,
   I did not rest till I could flip it backward,
   dance it on my tongue
   with a Miriam Makeba click.

I had no shame
   for the denial of my country
   or for the David West part of your name.

But now that you have gone to Africa
   (where I, too, surely, soon had better be)
   I face the test. You are truly there,
   I am absolutely here in wonderful Detroit.

And like a painter who has lost his sight,
   each time I inhale
   I realize the might
   that just seeing you here has been

And your "when we meet again in Africa"
   is dim. It fails to comfort me.
   It is Tamunoemi talking as he floats across wide seas.

So that when I try to call, your name
   starts clicking and flapping
   fluttering and rapping
   at the cage in my throat.

And DAVID is the word that rages through me.
   DAVID is the muttered note.
   And finally, trembling up and flying out comes
   DAVID.
   I wail.
   Hoping that your American name
   will draw you back to wonderful Detroit,

bringing again that power that formerly came
   from the use of Tamunoemi
   your African name.

The Slave and the Iron Lace

The craving of Samuel Rouse for clearance to create
was surely as hot as the iron that buffeted him. His pas-
   sion
for freedom so strong that it molded the smouldering
   fashions
he laced, for how also could a slave plot
or counterplot such incomparable shapes,

form or reform, for house after house,
the intricate Patio pattern, the delicate
Rose and Lyre, the Debutante Settee,
the complex but famous Grape; frame the classic vein
in an iron bench?

How could he turn an iron Venetian urn, wind the
   Grape Vine, chain
the trunk of a pine with a Round-the-Tree-settee,
mold a Floating Flower tray, a French chair—create all
   this
in such exquisite fairyland taste, that he'd be freed
and his skill would still resound a hundred years after?

And I wonder if I, with this thick asbestos glove of an
attitude could lace, forge and blend this ton of lead-
chained spleen surrounding me?
Could I manifest and sustain it into a new free-form
screen
of, not necessarily love, but (at the very least, for all
concerned) grace.

MARGARET WALKER (1915–   )

Street Demonstration

*"Hurry up Lucille or we won't get
arrested with our group."*
(AN EIGHT YEAR OLD DEMONSTRATOR, 1963)

We're hoping to be arrested
And hoping to go to jail
We'll sing and shout and pray
For Freedom and for Justice
And for Human Dignity
The fighting may be long
And some of us will die
But Liberty is costly
And ROME they say to me
Was not built in one day.

*Hurry up, Lucille, Hurry up
We're Going to Miss Our Chance to go to Jail.*

Girl Held Without Bail

*"In an unjust state the only place
for a just man is in jail."*

I like it here just fine
And I don't want no bail
My sister's here
My mother's here
And all my girl friends too.
I want my rights
I'm fighting for my rights

I want to be treated
Just like *anybody* else
I want to be treated
Just like *everybody* else

I like it fine in Jail
And I don't want no Bail.

For Malcolm X

All you violated ones with gentle hearts;
You violent dreamers whose cries shout heartbreak;
Whose voices echo clamors of our cool capers,
And whose black faces have hollowed pits for eyes.
All you gambling sons and hooked children and bowery
    bums
Hating white devils and black bourgeoisie,
Thumbing your noses at your burning red suns,
Gather round this coffin and mourn your dying swan.

Snow-white moslem head-dress around a dead black
    face!
Beautiful were your sand-papering words against our
    skins!
Our blood and water pour from your flowing wounds.
You have cut open our breasts and dug scalpels in our
    brains.
When and Where will another come to take your holy
    place?
Old man mumbling in his dotage, or crying child, unborn?

For Andy Goodman—
Michael Schwerner—
and James Chaney

(Three Civil Rights Workers
Murdered in Mississippi on June 21, 1964)

(Written After Seeing the Movie, *Andy In A.M.*)

Three faces . . .
    mirrored in the muddy streams of living . . .
young and tender like
quiet beauty of still water,
sensitive as the mimosa leaf,
    intense as the stalking cougar
    and impassive as the face of rivers;
The sensitive face of Andy
The intense face of Michael
The impassive face of Chaney.

Three leaves . . .
    Floating in the melted snow
    Flooding the Spring
    oak leaves
    one by one
    moving like a barge
    across the seasons
    moving like a breeze across the window pane
    winter . . . summer . . . spring
When is the evil year of the cricket?
When comes the violent day of the stone?
In which month
do the dead ones appear at the cistern?

Three lives . . .
    turning on the axis of our time
    Black and white together
    turning on the wheeling compass
    of a decade and a day
    The concerns of a century of time
    . . . an hourglass of destiny

Three lives . . .
   ripe for immortality of daisies and wheat
   for the simple beauty of a humming bird
   and dignity of a sequoia
   of renunciation and
   resurrection
For the Easter morning of our Meridians.

Why should another die for me?
Why should there be a calvary
A subterranean hell for three?
In the miry clay?
In the muddy stream?
In the red misery?
In mutilating hatred and in fear?
The brutish and the brazen
without brain
without blessing
without beauty . . .
They have killed these three.
They have killed them for me

Sunrise and sunset . . .
Spring rain and winter window pane . . .
I see the first leaves budding
The green Spring returning
I mark the falling
of golden Autumn leaves
and three lives floating down the quiet stream
Till they come to the surging falls . . .

The burned blossoms of the dogwood tree
tremble in the Mississippi morning
The wild call of the cardinal bird
troubles the Mississippi morning
I hear the morning singing
larks, robins, and the mocking bird
while the mourning dove
broods over the meadow
Summer leaf falls never turning brown

Deep in a Mississippi thicket
I hear that mourning dove
Bird of death singing in the swamp
Leaves of death floating in their watery grave

Three faces turn their ears and eyes
sensitive
intense
impassive
to see the solemn sky of summer
to hear the brooding cry
of the mourning dove

Mississippi bird of sorrow
O mourning bird of death
Sing their sorrow
Mourn their pain
And teach us death,
To love and live with them again!

Prophets for a New Day

1.

As the Word came to prophets of old,
As the burning bush spoke to Moses,
And the fiery coals cleansed the lips of Isaiah;
As the wheeling cloud in the sky
Clothed the message of Ezekiel;
So the Word of fire burns today
On the lips of our prophets in an evil age—
Our sooth-sayers and doom-tellers and doers of the Word.
So the Word of the Lord stirs again
These passionate people toward deliverance.
As Amos, Shepherd of Tekoa, spoke
To the captive children of Judah,
Preaching to the dispossessed and the poor,

So today in the pulpits and the jails,
On the highways and in the byways,
A fearless shepherd speaks at last
To his suffering weary sheep.

2.

So, kneeling by the river bank
Comes the vision to a valley of believers
So in flaming flags of stars in the sky
And in the breaking dawn of a blinding sun
The lamp of truth is lighted in the Temple
And the oil of devotion is burning at midnight
So the glittering censer in the Temple
Trembles in the presence of the priests
And the pillars of the door-posts move
And the incense rises in smoke
And the dark faces of the sufferers
Gleam in the new morning
The complaining faces glow
And the winds of freedom begin to blow
While the Word descends on the waiting World below.

3.

A beast is among us.
His mark is on the land.
His horns and his hands and his lips are gory with our
    blood.
He is War and Famine and Pestilence
He is Death and Destruction and Trouble
And he walks in our houses at noonday
And devours our defenders at midnight.
He is the demon who drives us with whips of fear
And in his cowardice
He cries out against liberty
He cries out against humanity
Against all dignity of green valleys and high hills
Against clean winds blowing through our living;
Against the broken bodies of our brothers.

He has crushed them with a stone.
He drinks our tears for water
And he drinks our blood for wine;
He eats our flesh like a ravenous lion
And he drives us out of the city
To be stabbed on a lonely hill.

RAY DUREM (1915–63)

I Know I'm Not Sufficiently Obscure

I know I'm not sufficiently obscure
to please the critics—nor devious enough.
Imagery escapes me.
I cannot find those mild and gracious words
to clothe the carnage.
Blood is blood and murder's murder.
What's a lavender word for lynch?
Come, you pale poets, wan, refined and dreamy:
here is a black woman working out her guts
in a white man's kitchen
for little money and no glory.
How should I tell that story?
There is a black boy, blacker still from death,
face down in the cold Korean mud.
Come on with your effervescent jive
explain to him why he ain't alive.
Reword our specific discontent
into some plaintive melody,
a little whine, a little whimper,
not too much—and no rebellion!
God, no! Rebellion's much too corny.
You deal with finer feelings,
very subtle—an autumn leaf
hanging from a tree—I see a body!

Award

*A Gold Watch to the FBI
Man who has followed
me for 25 years.*

Well, old spy
looks like I
led you down some pretty blind alleys,
took you on several trips to Mexico,
fishing in the high Sierras,
jazz at the Philharmonic.
You've watched me all your life,
I've clothed your wife,
put your two sons through college.
what good has it done?
the sun keeps rising every morning.
ever see me buy an Assistant President?
or close a school?
or lend money to Trujillo?
ever catch me rigging airplane prices?
I bought some after-hours whiskey in L.A.
but the Chief got his pay.
I ain't killed no Koreans
or fourteen-year-old boys in Mississippi.
neither did I bomb Guatemala,
or lend guns to shoot Algerians.
I admit I took a Negro child
to a white rest room in Texas,
but she was my daughter, only three,
who had to pee.

GWENDOLYN BROOKS (1917–   )

The Mother

Abortions will not let you forget.
You remember the children you got that you did not get,
The damp small pulps with a little or with no hair,
The singers and workers that never handled the air.
You will never neglect or beat
Them, or silence or buy with a sweet.
You will never wind up the sucking-thumb
Or scuttle off ghosts that come.
You will never leave them, controlling your luscious sigh,
Return for a snack of them, with gobbling mother-eye.

I have heard in the voices of the wind the voices of my
      dim killed children.
I have contracted. I have eased
My dim dears at the breasts they could never suck.
I have said, Sweets, if I sinned, if I seized
Your luck
And your lives from your unfinished reach,
If I stole your births and your names,
Your straight baby tears and your games,
Your stilted or lovely loves, your tumults, your marriages,
      aches, and your deaths,
If I poisoned the beginnings of your breaths,
Believe that even in my deliberateness I was not deliber-
      ate.
Though why should I whine,
Whine that the crime was other than mine?—
Since anyhow you are dead.
Or rather, or instead,
You were never made.
But that too, I am afraid,
Is faulty: oh, what shall I say, how is the truth to be
      said?

You were born, you had body, you died.
It is just that you never giggled or planned or cried.

Believe me, I loved you all.
Believe me, I knew you, though faintly, and I loved, I
    loved you
All.

Kitchenette Building

We are things of dry hours and the involuntary plan,
Grayed in, and gray. "Dream" makes a giddy sound, not
    strong
Like "rent," "feeding a wife," "satisfying a man."

But could a dream send up through onion fumes
Its white and violet, fight with fried potatoes
And yesterday's garbage ripening in the hall,
Flutter, or sing an aria down these rooms

Even if we were willing to let it in,
Had time to warm it, keep it very clean,
Anticipate a message, let it begin?

We wonder. But not well! not for a minute!
Since Number Five is out of the bathroom now,
We think of lukewarm water, hope to get in it.

What Shall I Give My Children?

What shall I give my children? who are poor,
Who are adjudged the leastwise of the land,
Who are my sweetest lepers, who demand
No velvet and no velvety velour;
But who have begged me for a brisk contour,
Crying that they are quasi, contraband

Because unfinished, graven by a hand
Less than angelic, admirable or sure.
My hand is stuffed with mode, design, device.
But I lack access to my proper stone.
And plenitude of plan shall not suffice
Nor grief nor love shall be enough alone
To ratify my little halves who bear
Across an autumn freezing everywhere.

The Rites for Cousin Vit

Carried her unprotesting out the door.
Kicked back the casket-stand. But it can't hold her,
That stuff and satin aiming to enfold her,
The lid's contrition nor the bolts before.
Oh oh. Too much. Too much. Even now, surmise,
She rises in the sunshine. There she goes,
Back to the bars she knew and the repose
In love-rooms and the things in people's eyes.
Too vital and too squeaking. Must emerge.
Even now she does the snake-hips with a hiss,
Slops the bad wine across her shantung, talks
Of pregnancy, guitars and bridgework, walks
In parks or alleys, comes haply on the verge
Of happiness, haply hysterics. Is.

A Lovely Love

Let it be alleys. Let it be a hall
Whose janitor javelins epithet and thought
To cheapen hyacinth darkness that we sought
And played we found, rot, make the petals fall.
Let it be stairways, and a splintery box
Where you have thrown me, scraped me with your kiss,
Have honed me, have released me after this
Cavern kindness, smiled away our shocks.

That is the birthright of our lovely love
In swaddling clothes. Not like that Other one.
Not lit by any fondling star above.
Not found by any wise men, either. Run.
People are coming. They must not catch us here
Definitionless in this strict atmosphere.

When You Have Forgotten Sunday: The Love Story

——And when you have forgotten the bright bedclothes
   on a Wednesday and a Saturday,
And most especially when you have forgotten Sunday—
When you have forgotten Sunday halves in bed,
Or me sitting on the front-room radiator in the limping
   afternoon
Looking off down the long street
To nowhere,
Hugged by my plain old wrapper of no-expectation
And nothing-I-have-to-do and I'm-happy-why?
And if-Monday-never-had-to-come—
When you have forgotten that, I say,
And how you swore, if somebody beeped the bell,
And how my heart played hopscotch if the telephone
   rang;
And how we finally went in to Sunday dinner,
That is to say, went across the front room floor to the
   ink-spotted table in the southwest corner
To Sunday dinner, which was always chicken and
   noodles
Or chicken and rice
And salad and rye bread and tea
And chocolate chip cookies—
I say, when you have forgotten that,
When you have forgotten my little presentiment
That the war would be over before they got to you;
And how we finally undressed and whipped out the
   light and flowed into bed,
And lay loose-limbed for a moment in the week-end

Bright bedclothes,
Then gently folded into each other—
When you have, I say, forgotten all that,
Then you may tell,
Then I may believe
You have forgotten me well.

The Chicago Picasso

August 15, 1967

> "Mayor Daley tugged a white ribbon,
> loosing the blue percale wrap. A hearty cheer
> went up as the covering slipped off the big
> steel sculpture that looks at once like a
> bird and a woman."
>
> —CHICAGO SUN-TIMES

*(Seiji Ozawa leads the Symphony.
The Mayor smiles.
And 50,000 See.)*

Does man love Art? Man visits Art, but squirms.
Art hurts. Art urges voyages—
and it is easier to stay at home,
the nice beer ready.
          In commonrooms
we belch, or sniff, or scratch.
Are raw.

But we must cook ourselves and style ourselves for Art,
    who
is a requiring courtesan.
We squirm.
We do not hug the Mona Lisa.
We
may touch or tolerate
an astounding fountain, or a horse-and-rider.
At most, another Lion.

Observe the tall cold of a Flower
which is as innocent and as guilty,
as meaningful and as meaningless as any
other flower in the western field.

The Sermon on the Warpland

> "The fact that we are black
> is our ultimate reality."
> —RON KARENGA

And several strengths from drowsiness campaigned
but spoke in Single Sermon on the warpland.

And went about the warpland saying No.
"My people, black and black, revile the River.
Say that the River turns, and turn the River.

Say that our Something in doublepod contains
seeds for the coming hell and health together.
Prepare to meet
(sisters, brothers) the brash and terrible weather;
the pains;
the bruising; the collapse of bestials, idols.
But then oh then!—the stuffing of the hulls!
the seasoning of the periously sweet!
the health! the heralding of the clear obscure!

Build now your Church, my brothers, sisters. Build
never with brick nor Corten nor with granite.
Build with lithe love. With love like lion-eyes.
With love like morningrise.
With love like black, our black—
luminously indiscreet;
complete; continuous."

The Second Sermon on the Warpland

For Walter Bradford

1.

This is the urgency: Live!
and have your blooming in the noise of the whirlwind.

2.

Salve salvage in the spin.
Endorse the splendor splashes;
stylize the flawed utility;
prop a malign or failing light—
but know the whirlwind is our commonwealth.
Not the easy man, who rides above them all,
not the jumbo brigand,
not the pet bird of poets, that sweetest sonnet,
shall straddle the whirlwind.
Nevertheless, live.

3.

All about are the cold places,
all about are the pushmen and jeopardy, theft—
all about are the stormers and scramblers but
what must our Season be, which starts from Fear?
Live and go out.
Define and
medicate the whirlwind.

4.

The time
cracks into furious flower. Lifts its face
all unashamed. And sways in wicked grace.
Whose half-black hands assemble oranges
is tom-tom hearted
(goes in bearing oranges and boom).
And there are bells for orphans—
and red and shriek and sheen.

A garbageman is dignified
as any diplomat.
Big Bessie's feet hurt like nobody's business,
but she stands—bigly—under the unruly scrutiny, stands
    in the wild weed.

In the wild weed
she is a citizen,
and is a moment of highest quality; admirable.

It is lonesome, yes. For we are the last of the loud.
Nevertheless, live.

Conduct your blooming in the noise and whip of the
    whirlwind.

YOUNG HEROES

I

Keorapetse Kgositsile (Willie)

He is very busy with his looking.
To look, he knows, is to involve
subject and suppliant.
He looks at life—
moves life into his hands—
saying
Art is life worked with: is life
wheedled, or whelmed:
assessed:
clandestine, but evoked.

Look! Look to *this* page!
A horror here
walks toward you in working clothes.
    He sees
hellishness among the half-men.

He sees
pellmelling loneliness in the
center of grouphood.
He sees
lenient dignity. He
sees pretty flowers under blood.

He teaches dolls and dynamite.
Because he knows
there is a scientific thinning of our ranks.
Not merely Medgar Malcolm Martin and Black Panthers,
but Susie. Cecil Williams. Azzie Jane.
He teaches
strategy and the straight aim;
black volume;
might of mind, black flare—
volcanoing merit, black
herohood.

Black total.

        He is no kitten Traveler
and no poor Knower of himself.

        Blackness
is a going to essences and to unifyings.

"MY NAME IS AFRIKA"!
        Well, every fella's a Foreign Country.

This Foreign Country speaks to You.

II

To Don at Salaam

I like to see you lean back in your chair
so far you have to fall but do not—
your arms back, your fine hands
in your print pockets.

Beautiful. Impudent.
Ready for life.
A tied storm.

I like to see you wearing your boy smile
whose tribute is for two of us or three.

Sometimes in life
things seem to be moving
and they are not
and they are not
there.
You are there.

Your voice is the listened-for music.
Your act is the consolation.

I like to see you living in the world.

III

Walter Bradford

Just As You Think You're "Better Now"
Something Comes To The Door.
It's a Wilderness, Walter.
It's a Whirlpool or Whipper.

THEN you have to revise the messages;
and, pushing through roars of the Last Trombones of
    seduction,
the deft orchestration,
settle the sick ears to hear and to heed and to hold;
the sick ears a-plenty.

It's Walter-work, Walter.
——Not overmuch for
brick-fitter, brick-MAKER, and wave-
outwitter;
whip-stopper.

Not overmuch for a
Tree-planting Man.

Stay.

RIOT

Riot

> A riot is the language of the unheard
> —MARTIN LUTHER KING

John Cabot, out of Wilma, once a Wycliffe,
all whitebluerose below his golden hair,
wrapped richly in right linen and right wool,
almost forgot his Jaguar and Lake Bluff;
almost forgot Grandtully (which is The
Best Thing That Ever Happened To Scotch); almost
forgot the sculpture at the Richard Gray
and Distelheim; the kidney pie at Maxim's,
the *Grenadine de Boeuf* at Maison Henri.

Because the Negroes were coming down the street.

Because the Poor were sweaty and unpretty
(not like Two Dainty Negroes in Winnetka)
and they were coming toward him in rough ranks.
In seas. In windsweep. They were black and loud.
And not detainable. And not discreet.

Gross. Gross. "*Que tu es grossier!*" John Cabot
itched instantly beneath the nourished white
that told his story of glory to the World.
"Don't let It touch me! the blackness! Lord!" he whis-
    pered
to any handy angel in the sky.

But, in a thrilling announcement, on It drove
and breathed on him: and touched him. In that breath
the fume of pig foot, chitterling and cheap chili,
malign, mocked John. And, in terrific touch, old
averted doubt jerked forward decently,
cried "Cabot! John! You are a desperate man,
and the desperate die expensively today."

John Cabot went down in the smoke and fire
and broken glass and blood, and he cried "Lord!
Forgive these nigguhs that know not what they do."

The Third Sermon on the Warpland

> Phoenix
> "In Egyptian mythology, a bird which
> lived for five hundred years and then
> consumed itself in fire, rising renewed
> from the ashes."
>
> —WEBSTER

The earth is a beautiful place.
Watermirrors and things to be reflected.
Goldenrod across the little lagoon.

The Black Philosopher says
"Our chains are in the keep of the Keeper
in a labeled cabinet
on the second shelf by the cookies,
sonatas, the arabesques . . . .
There's a rattle, sometimes.
You do not hear it who mind only
cookies and crunch them.
You do not hear the remarkable music—'A
Death Song For You Before You Die.'
If you could hear it
you would make music too.
The *black*blues."

West Madison Street.
In "Jessie's Kitchen"
nobody's eating Jessie's Perfect Food.
Crazy flowers
cry up across the sky, spreading
and hissing *This is*
it.

The young men run.

They will not steal Bing Crosby but will steal
Melvin Van Peebles who made Lillie
a thing of Zampoughi a thing of red wiggles and trebles
(and I know there are twenty wire stalks sticking out of
   her head
as her underfed haunches jerk jazz).

A clean riot is not one in which little rioters
long-stomped, long-straddled, BEANLESS
but knowing no Why
go steal in hell
a radio, sit to hear James Brown
and Mingus, Young-Holt, Coleman, John, on V.O.N.,
and sun themselves in Sin.

However, what
is going on
is going on.

Fire.
That is their way of lighting candles in the darkness.
A White Philosopher said
"It is better to light one candle than curse the darkness."
      These candles curse—
inverting the deeps of the darkness.

GUARD HERE, GUNS LOADED.
The young men run.

The children in ritual chatter
scatter upon
their Own and old geography.

The Law comes sirening across the town.

A woman is dead.
Motherwoman.
She lies among the boxes
(that held the haughty hats, the Polish sausages)
in newish, thorough, firm virginity
as rich as fudge is if you've had five pieces.
Not again shall she
partake of steak
on Christmas mornings, nor of nighttime
chicken and wine at Val Gray Ward's
nor say
of Mr. Beetley, Exit Jones, Junk Smith
nor neat New-baby Williams (man-to-many)
"He treat me right."

That was a gut gal.

"We'll do an us!" yells Yancey, a twittering twelve.
"Instead of your deathintheafternoon,
kill 'em, bull!
kill 'em, bull!"

The Black Philosopher blares
"I tell you, ex*haust*ive black integrity
would assure a blackless America . . . . "

Nine die, Sun-Times will tell
and will tell too
in small black-bordered oblongs "*Rumor? check it
at 744–4111.*"

A Poem to Peanut.
"Cooooooool!" purrs Peanut. Peanut is
Richard—a Ranger and a gentleman.

A Signature. A Herald. And a Span.
This Peanut will not let his men explode.
And Rico will not.
Neither will Sengali.
Nor Bop nor Jeff, Geronimo nor Lover.
These merely peer and purr,
and pass the Passion over.
The Disciples stir
and thousandfold confer
with ranging Rangermen;
mutual in their "Yeah!—
this AIN'T all upinheah!"

"But WHY do These People offend *themselves?*" say they
who say also "It's time.
It's time to help
These People."

Lies are told and legends made.
Phoenix rises unafraid.

The Black Philosopher will remember:
"There they came to life and exulted,
the hurt mute.
Then it was over.

The dust, as they say, settled."

An Aspect of Love, Alive in the Ice and Fire

LABOHEM BROWN

In a package of minutes there is this We.
How beautiful.
Merry foreigners in our morning,
we laugh, we touch each other,
are responsible props and posts.

A physical light is in the room.

Because the world is at the window
we cannot wonder very long.

You rise. Although
genial, you are in yourself again.
I observe
your direct and respectable stride.
You are direct and self-accepting as a lion
in African velvet. You are level, lean, remote.

There is a moment in Camaraderie
when interruption is not to be understood.
I cannot bear an interruption.
This is the shining joy;
the time of not-to-end.

On the street we smile.
We go
in different directions
down the imperturbable street.

The Nineteen Sixties

SOS

Calling black people
Calling all black people, man woman child
Wherever you are, calling you, urgent, come in
Black People, come in, wherever you are, urgent, calling
you, calling all black people
calling all black people, come in, black people, come
on in.

IMAMU AMIRI BARAKA

MARI EVANS

Black jam for dr negro

Pullin me in off the corner to wash my face an
cut my afro turn
my collar
down
when that aint my
thang I
walk heels first
nose round an tilted
up
my ancient
eyes
see your thang
baby
an it aint
shit
your thang
puts my eyes out baby
turns my seeking fingers
    into splintering fists
messes up my head
and I scream you out
your thang
is whats wrong
    an you keep
    pilin it on rubbin it
    in
    smoothly doin it
    to death

what you sweatin
baby
    your guts

puked and rotten
waitin
to be
    defended

To Mother and Steve

All I wanted
was your
love

when I rolled down
Brewster blew
soft pot clouds on
subs when
I lay in nameless rooms
cold-sweating
horse in nameless arms
crawled
thru white hell owning
no one no one no one save
one purple-bruised soul
pawned
in exchange for
oblivion
    all I wanted
was
your love

not twice but
constantly
I tried
to free you
it was all
such cold shit
then
the last day

of the
last year
of my raw-edged anguish
I was able wearily
at last—
to roll.

(all I wanted
was
your love)
I bought this final
battered gift

(do not refuse—for it
was all
I had)

with my back supported
by the tolerant
arms
of a picket fence and my
legs crumpled crazily in front
and love fell
soft and cold and
covered me in
blanket
like
the one you
tucked around me
centuries
ago and like that
later
lifted gently
o'er my face
and in this season
of peace and
goodwill and the smell
of cedar
remembered

thru warm yellow
windows—
    all I wanted
and it was more than
I could stand and
more than a thousand passions and
I could not
mainline it
away . . .
    was your
    love

Spectrum

Petulance is purple
happiness pink
ennui chartreuse
and love
—I think
is blue
like midnight sometimes
or a robin's egg
sometimes

Where Have You Gone

Where have you gone

with your confident
walk with
your crooked smile

why did you leave
me
when you took your
laughter
and departed

are you aware that
with you
went the sun
all light
and what few stars
there were?

where have you gone
with your confident
walk your
crooked smile the
rent money
in one pocket and
my heart
in another . . .

Marrow of My Bone

Fondle me
caress
and cradle
me
with your lips
withdraw
the nectar from
me
teach me there
is
someone

JAMES EMANUEL (1921–   )

Nightmare

From deep sleep
I sat upright
And clutched his new lapels,

For he was laughing.
Back from the dead
He came, I say,
Laughing.

I asked not
"Are you not dead?"
But
"What *is* it?"

His talcum chin,
And pebble eyes,
And old string hair
Leaned forward.

He just laughed.
He just laughed
At my tears.

The Negro

Never saw him.
Never can.
Hypothetical,
Haunting man:

Eyes a-saucer,
Yessir bossir,
Dice a-clicking,
Razor flicking.

The-ness froze him
In a dance.
A-ness never
Had a chance.

Negritude

Black is the first nail I ever stepped on;
Black the hand that dried my tears.
Black is the first old man I ever noticed;
Black the burden of his years.

Black is waiting in the darkness;
Black the ground where hoods have lain.
Black is the sorrow-misted story;
Black the brotherhood of pain.

Black is a quiet iron door;
Black the path that leads behind.
Black is a detour through the years;
Black the diary of the mind.

Black is Gabriel Prosser's knuckles;
Black Sojourner's naked breast.
Black is a schoolgirl's breathless mother;
Black her child who led the rest.

Black is the purring of a motor;
Black the foot when the light turns green.
Black is last year's dusty paper;
Black the headlines yet unseen.

Black is a burden bravely chanted:
Black cross of sweat for a nation's rise.
Black is a boy who knows his heroes;
Black the way a hero dies.

The Treehouse

To every man
His treehouse,
A green splice in the humping years,
Spartan with narrow cot
And prickly door.

To every man
His twilight flash
Of luminous recall
    of tiptoe years
    in leaf-stung flight;
    of days of squirm and bite
    that waved antennas through the grass;
    of nights
    when every moving thing
    was girlshaped,
    expectantly turning.

To every man
His house below
And his house above—
With perilous stairs
Between.

For "Mr. Dudley," a Black Spy

Halem dud,
pulpit spoiler of the Word,
shapeshifter faking cards,
credentials slicking up whatever role
Master Whitey Big
kicked on you: painter,
preacher, plumber,
butt-hustler reeking,

I saw you
hear you lisping cute
for Adam, tricking Clayton
fooling Powell, fronting cameras
that choked that big white collar round your neck,
you strangling,
spit missing Bimini.

I saw you
know you mixing Judas paint
with Judas praise when you pushed in
that startled woman's door,
with "Mr. Dudley" on your card
and in your peeling mind already Judas pipes
installed to plumb, to bug the private hearts,
to taptape fireside beside table talk—
her family Black but not your kind,
below their Afros
cheekless for your kiss.

I saw you
remember you mixing in, slick-
fingering the campus Blacks,
taptapping on Columbia shoulders,
systemshakers not startled by you,
uncle, old jitterbug slobbering young jive,
sidling sleeve-tugger, lisping
for inside dope, hustling Harlem filter tips
and names to trade on.

For you, "Dudley,"
and your beardless, baubled clan,
these loathings
to suck on.

Panther Man

Wouldnt think
t look at m
he was so damn bad
they had t sneak up on m,
shoot m in his head
in his bed
sleepin
Afroed up 3 inches
smilin gunpowder.

Hey, Mister Panther!
Get up
and fight that cracker-back,
back m gainst the wall
of YOUR room
where YOU sleep
with YOUR dreams
and take down his goddam name
take down his goddam number
give m a motel napkin
to hold the blood
where YOUR bullet
grabbed m,
tell m YOUR name
YOUR race
make m write it down
in HIS blood
for HIS momma to remember,
back m out yr door
and make m come in RIGHT—
in daylight

with ALL his pukey buddies
behind guns cursin Black men,
makin gut noises
wakin up the WORLD.

Tell m, Panther!
Get up out yr dead bed;
if THATS the way he is
even yr GHOST
can take m.

NAOMI MADGETT (1923–)

Quest

I will track you down the years,
    Down the night,
Till my anguish falls away,
    Star by star,
And my heart spreads flaming wings
    Where you are.

I will find you, never fear—
    Make you mine.
Think that you have bound me fast
    To the earth?
I will rise to sing you yet,
    Song of mirth.

I will let you think you won,
    Perfect dream,
Till I creep from dark and toil
    To your side,
Hold you to my heart and sleep,
    Satisfied.

I will track you down the sky,
    Down the blue,
Till my song becomes the sun
    Of the years
And the golden April rains
    Are my tears.

Star Journey

Alone I tiptoe through the stars,
Precipitously steep,
Watchful lest I wake the gods
And angels from their sleep.

Alone I climb the secret hills
Unknown to mortal feet
And stand upon a peak where you
And I can never meet.

To you who do not dream, I am
A gently tilted head,
A voice that chatters, earth-aware,
A gay mouth painted red.

Better that you possess a cold
Impenetrable stone
Than woo my body while my soul
Tips through the stars alone.

Dream Sequence, Part 9

Was it really you all the time?
You who first stumbled upon me
Behind some sea-soaked rock?
Or was it I who, first surprised to find you there,
Came running then through the salt wind,
Feet wet, hair flying?

Who opened the door?
Who entered first and which one followed?
Out of breath, out of mind, I woke
In the house somebody built of crusted sand.
(To trap us or to give us peace, or both?)
I never knew but thought I knew *I* built it
And led you there.
Was it you?

The Race Question

*(For one whose fame depends on keeping
The Problem a problem)*

Would it please you if I strung my tears
In pearls for you to wear?
Would you like a gift of my hands' endless beating
Against old bars?

This time I can forget my Otherness,
Silence my drums of discontent awhile
And listen to the stars.

Wait in the shadows if you choose.
Stand alert to catch
The thunder and first sprinkle of unrest
Your insufficiency demands,
But you will find no comfort.
I will not feed your hunger with my blood
Nor crown your nakedness
With jewels of my elegant pain.

Pavlov

Unless you remind me,
Unless you ring the bell,
I might forget the hang-dog, mad-dog
Militant response,
Mightn't I?

Is it this that makes you stand
A distance off
Afraid,
Because you find me dangerously
Independently
Passive?

Midway

I've come this far to freedom and I won't turn back.
I'm climbing to the highway from my old dirt track.
    I'm coming and I'm going
    And I'm stretching and I'm growing
And I'll reap what I've been sowing or my skin's not
   black.

I've prayed and slaved and waited and I've sung my
   song.
You've bled me and you've starved me but I've still
   grown strong.
    You've lashed me and you've treed me
    And you've everything but freed me
But in time you'll know you need me and it won't be
   long.

I've seen the daylight breaking high above the bough.
I've found my destination and I've made my vow;
    So whether you abhor me
    Or deride me or ignore me,
Mighty mountains loom before me and I won't stop now.

Alabama Centennial

They said, "Wait." Well, I waited.
For a hundred years I waited
In cotton fields, kitchens, balconies,
In bread lines, at back doors, on chain gangs,
In stinking "colored" toilets
And crowded ghettos,
Outside of schools and voting booths.
And some said, "Later."
And some said, "Never!"

Then a new wind blew, and a new voice
Rode its wings with quiet urgency,

Strong, determined, sure.
"No," it said. "Not 'never,' not 'later,'
Not even 'soon.'
Now.
Walk!"

And other voices echoed the freedom words,
"Walk together, children, don't get weary,"
Whispered them, sang them, prayed them, shouted them.
"Walk!"
And I walked the streets of Montgomery
Until a link in the chain of patient acquiescence broke.

Then again: Sit down!
And I sat down at the counters of Greensboro.
Ride! And I rode the bus for freedom.
Kneel! And I went down on my knees in prayer and
    faith.
March! And I'll march until the last chain falls
Singing, "We shall overcome."

Not all the dogs and hoses in Birmingham
Nor all the clubs and guns in Selma
Can turn this tide.
Not all the jails can hold these young black faces
From their destiny of manhood,
Of equality, of dignity,
Of the American Dream
A hundred years past due.
Now!

CONRAD KENT RIVERS (1933–68)

A Mourning Letter from Paris

(for Richard Wright)

All night I walked among your spirits, Richard:
the Paris you adored is most politely dead.

I found French-speaking bigots and some sterile blacks,
bright African boys forgetting their ancestral robes,
a few men of color seeking the same French girl.

Polished Americans watched the stark reality
of mass integration, pretending not to look homeward
where the high ground smelled of their daughters' death.

I searched for the skin of your bones, Richard.
Mississippi called you back to her genuine hard clay,
but here one finds a groove, adapts, then lingers on.

For me, my good dead friend of searing words
and thirsty truth, the road to Paris leads back home:
one gets to miss the stir of Harlem's honeyed voice,
or one forgets the joy to which we were born.

Four Sheets to the Wind
and a One-Way Ticket to France

As a child
I bought a red scarf and women told me
                how beautiful it looked.
Wandering through the sous-sols as France
                wandered through me.

In the evenings
I would watch the funny people make love
                              the way Maupassant said.
My youth allowed me the opportunity to hear
                              all those strange
verbs conjugated in erotic affirmation. I knew love at
    twelve.

When Selassie went before his peers and Dillinger goofed
I read in two languages, not really caring which one
                              belonged to me.

My mother lit a candle for George, my father
                              went broke, we died.
When I felt blue, the Champs understood, and when
                              it was crowded
the alley behind Harry's New York Bar soothed
                              my restless spirit.

I liked to watch the nonconformists gaze at the paintings
along Gauguin's bewildered paradise.

Braque once passed me in front of the Cafe Musique.
I used to watch those sneaky professors examine the
    populace.
Americans never quite fitted in, but they tried so we
    smiled.

In Defense of Black Poets

(for Hoyt)

The critics cry unfair
      yet the poem is born.
Some black emancipated baby
      will scratch his head
wondering why you felt compelled
      to say whatever you said.

A black poet must bear in mind
    the misery.
The color-seekers fear poems
    they can't buy for a ten-dollar
bill or with a clever contract.
    Some black kid is bound to read you.

A black poet must remember the horrors.
    The good jobs can't last forever.
It shall come to pass that the fury
    of a token revolution will fade
into the bank accounts of countless blacks
    and freedom-loving whites.

The brilliant novels shall pass
    into the archives of a 'keep cool
we've done enough for you' generation:
    the movement organizations already
await their monthly checks from Downtown
    and

only the forgotten wails of a few black
    poets and artists
shall survive the then of then,
    the now of now.

The Death of a Negro Poet

(preludes)

I

In a few moments
the song will set me free,
but the yearning returns.

Free? Is that to be alone
remembering loves of yesterday,
look beyond home?

Apart from you, I mourn
over the face of me and night,
thanking the nothing of all.

And if my street flows to Paris,
I return home. Sudden worlds are small.
My transitions are frequent withdrawals.

Distance and silence may not set us free,
yet I shall follow still water tides, lingering
in quest for soft new things inside of me.

II

Still waters be mine.
Cold grey stones let me be.
Something more than rock alone
seeking a black destiny.

Still waters be mine.
I long for the simple past.
Pity this dark child of time
embracing his fateful caste.

Still waters be mine.
Let my cup flow once again.
Give me the strength I need
searching the living end

or return the scolding promise
to wish me safe love again.

ETHERIDGE KNIGHT (1933–   )

The Idea of Ancestry

1

Taped to the wall of my cell are 47 pictures: 47 black
faces: my father, mother, grandmothers (1 dead), grand
fathers (both dead), brothers, sisters, uncles, aunts,
cousins (1st & 2nd), nieces, and nephews. They stare
across the space at me sprawling on my bunk. I know
their dark eyes, they know mine. I know their style,
they know mine. I am all of them, they are all of me;
they are farmers, I am a thief, I am me, they are thee.

I have at one time or another been in love with my
    mother,
1 grandmother, 2 sisters, 2 aunts (1 went to the asylum),
and 5 cousins. I am now in love with a 7 yr old niece
(she sends me letters written in large block print, and
her picture is the only one that smiles at me).

I have the same name as 1 grandfather, 3 cousins, 3
    nephews,
and 1 uncle. The uncle disappeared when he was 15, just
    took
off and caught a freight (they say). He's discussed each
    year
when the family has a reunion, he causes uneasiness in
the clan, he is an empty space. My father's mother, who
    is 93
and who keeps the Family Bible with everybody's birth
    dates
(and death dates) in it, always mentions him. There is
    no
place in her Bible for "whereabouts unknown."

2

Each Fall the graves of my grandfathers call me, the
brown
hills and red gullies of mississippi send out their electric
messages, galvanizing my genes. Last yr/like a salmon
quitting
the cold ocean—leaping and bucking up his birthstream/
I
hitchhiked my way from L.A. with 16 caps in my pocket
and a
monkey on my back. And I almost kicked it with the
kinfolks.
I walked barefooted in my grandmother's backyard/I
smelled the old
land and the woods/I sipped cornwhiskey from fruit jars
with the men/
I flirted with the women/I had a ball till the caps ran out
and my habit came down. That night I looked at my
grandmother
and split/my guts were screaming for junk/but I was al-
most
contented/I had almost caught up with me.
(The next day in Memphis I cracked a croaker's crib for
a fix.)

This yr there is a gray stone wall damming my stream,
and when
the falling leaves stir my genes, I pace my cell or flop
on my bunk
and stare at 47 black faces across the space. I am all of
them,
they are all of me, I am me, they are thee, and I have no
sons
to float in the space between.

For Freckle-Faced Gerald

Now you take ol Rufus. He beat drums,
was free and funky under the arms,
fucked white girls, jumped off a bridge
(and thought nothing of the sacrilege),
he copped out—and he was over twenty-one.

Take Gerald. Sixteen years hadn't even done
a good job on his voice. He didn't even know
how to talk tough, or how to hide the glow
of life before he was thrown in as "pigmeat"
for the buzzards to eat.

Gerald, who had no memory or hope of copper hot lips—
of firm upthrusting thighs
to reenforce his flow,
let tall walls and buzzards change the course
of his river from south to north.

(No safety in number like back on the block.
two's aplenty. three? definitely not.
four? "you're all muslims."
five? "you were planning a race riot."
plus, Gerald could never quite win
with his precise speech and innocent grin
the trust and fists of the young black cats.)

Gerald, sun-kissed ten thousand times on the nose
and cheeks, didn't stand a chance,
didn't even know that the loss of his balls
had been plotted years in advance
by wiser and bigger buzzards than those
who now hover above his track
and at night light upon his back.

Haiku

1

Eastern guard tower
glints in sunset; convicts rest
like lizards on rocks.

2

The piano man
is sting at 3 am
his songs drop like plum.

3

Morning sun slants cell.
Drunks stagger like cripple flies
On Jailhouse floor.

4

To write a blues song
is to regiment riots
and pluck gems from graves.

5

A bare pecan tree
slips a pencil shadow down
a moonlit snow slope.

6

The falling snow flakes
Can not blunt the hard aches nor
Match the steel stillness.

7

Under moon shadows
A tall boy flashes knife and
Slices star bright ice.

8

In the August grass
Struck by the last rays of sun
The cracked teacup screams.

9

Making jazz swing in
Seventeen syllables AIN'T
No square poet's job.

It Was a Funky Deal

It was a funky deal.
The only thing real was red,
Red blood around his red, red beard.

It was a funky deal.

In the beginning was the word,
And in the end the deed.
Judas did it to Jesus
For the same Herd. Same reason.
You made them mad, Malcolm. Same reason.

It was a funky deal.

You rocked too many boats, man.
Pulled too many coats, man.
Saw through the jive.
You reached the wild guys
Like me. You and Bird. (And that
Lil LeRoi cat.)

It was a funky deal.

The Violent Space
(*or when your sister sleeps around for money*)

Exchange in greed the ungraceful signs. Thrust
The thick notes between green apple breasts.
Then the shadow of the devil descends,
The violent space cries and angel eyes,
Large and dark, retreat in innocence and in ice.
(Run sister run—the Bugga man comes!)

The violent space cries silently,
Like you cried wide years ago
In another space, speckled by the sun
And the leaves of a green plum tree,
And you were stung
By a red wasp and we flew home.
(Run sister run—the Bugga man comes!)

Well, hell, lil sis, wasps still sting.
You are all of seventeen and as alone now
In your pain as you were with the sting
On your brow.
Well, shit, lil sis, here we are:
You and I and this poem.
And what should I do? should I squat
In the dust and make strange markings on the ground?
Shall I chant a spell to drive the demon away?
(Run sister run—the Bugga man comes!)

In the beginning you were the Virgin Mary,
And you are the Virgin Mary now.
But somewhere between Nazareth and Bethlehem
You lost your name in the nameless void.
O Mary don't you weep don't you moan
O Mary shake your butt to the violent juke,
Absorb the demon puke and watch the white eyes pop.
(Run sister run—the Bugga man comes!)

And what do I do? I boil my tears in a twisted spoon
And dance like an angel on the point of a needle.
I sit counting syllables like Midas gold.
I am not bold. I can not yet take hold of the demon
And lift his weight from your black belly,
So I grab the air and sing my song.
(But the air can not stand my singing long.)

I Sing of Shine

And, yeah, brothers,
while white/america sings about the unsink
able molly brown
(who was hustling the titanic
when it went down)
I sing to thee of Shine
the stoker who was hip
enough to flee the fucking ship
and let the white folks drown
with screams on their lips
(jumped his black ass into the dark sea, Shine did,
broke free from the straining steel.
yeah, I sing of Shine
and how the millionaire banker stood on the deck
and pulled from his pocket a million dollar check
saying Shine Shine save poor me
and I'll give you all the money a black boy needs—
how Shine looked at the money and then at the sea
and said jump in muthafucka and swim like me—
and Shine swam on—Shine swam on—
how the banker's daughter ran naked on the deck
with her pinktits trembling and her pants roun her neck
screaming Shine Shine save poor me
and I'll give you all the cunt a black boy needs—
how Shine said now cunt is good and that's no jive
but you got to swim not fuck to stay alive—
then Shine swam past a preacher afloat on a board

crying save me nigger Shine in the name of the Lord—
how the preacher grabbed Shine's arm and broke his
    stroke—
how Shine pulled his shank and cut the preacher's
    throat—
and Shine swam on—all alone.
And when the news hit shore that the titanic had sunk
Shine was up in Harlem damn near drunk—
and dancing in the streets.
yeah, damn near drunk and dancing in the streets.

IMAMU AMIRI BARAKA (1934–   )

An Agony. As now.

I am inside someone
who hates me. I look
out from his eyes. Smell
what fouled tunes come in
to his breath. Love his
wretched women.

Slits in the metal, for sun. Where
my eyes sit turning, at the cool air
the glance of light, or hard flesh
rubbed against me, a woman, a man,
without shadow, or voice, or meaning.

This is the enclosure (flesh,
where innocence is a weapon. An
abstraction. Touch. (Not mine.
Or yours, if you are the soul I had
and abandoned when I was blind and had
my enemies carry me as a dead man
(if he is beautiful, or pitied.

It can be pain. (As now, as all his
flesh hurts me.) It can be that. Or
pain. As when she ran from me into
that forest.
                    Or pain, the mind
silver spiraled whirled against the
sun, higher than even old men thought
God would be. Or pain. And the other. The
yes. (Inside his books, his fingers. They
are withered yellow flowers and were never
beautiful.) The yes. You will, lost soul, say

'beauty.' Beauty, practiced, as the tree. The
slow river. A white sun in its wet sentences.

Or, the cold men in their gale. Ecstasy. Flesh
or souls. The yes. (Their robes blown. Their bowls
empty. They chant at my heels, not at yours.) Flesh
or soul, as corrupt. Where the answer moves too quickly.
Where the God is a self, after all.)

Cold air blown through narrow blind eyes. Flesh,
white hot metal. Glows as the day with its sun.
It is a human love, I live inside. A bony skeleton
you recognize as words or simple feeling.

But it has no feeling. As the metal, is hot, it is not,
given to love.

It burns the thing
inside it. And that thing
screams.

The Pressures.

(Love twists
the young man. Having seen it
only once. He expected it
to be, as the orange flower
leather of the poet's book.
He expected
less hurt, a lyric. And not
the slow effortless pain
as a new dripping sun pushes
up out of our river.)

And
having seen it, refuses
to inhale. "It was a
green mist, seemed
to lift and choke
the town."

Ka 'Ba

A closed window looks down
on a dirty courtyard, and black people
call across or scream across or walk across
defying physics in the stream of their will

Our world is full of sound
Our world is more lovely than anyone's
tho we suffer, and kill each other
and sometimes fail to walk the air

We are beautiful people
with african imaginations
full of masks and dances and swelling chants
with african eyes, and noses, and arms,
though we sprawl in grey chains in a place
full of winters, when what we want is sun.

We have been captured,
brothers. And we labor
to make our getaway, into
the ancient image, into a new

correspondence with ourselves
and our black family. We need magic
now we need the spells, to raise up
return, destroy, and create. What will be

the sacred words?

Beautiful Black Women ...

Beautiful black women, fail, they act. Stop them, raining.
They are so beautiful, we want them with us. Stop them,
    raining.
Beautiful, stop raining, they fail. We fail them and their
    lips

stick out perpetually, at our weakness. Raining. Stop
them. Black
queens, Ruby Dee weeps at the window, raining, being
lost in her
life, being what we all will be, sentimental bitter frus-
trated
deprived of her fullest light. Beautiful black women, it is
still raining in this terrible land. We need you. We flex
our
muscles, turn to stare at our tormentor, we need you.
Raining.
We need you, reigning, black queen. This/terrible black
ladies
wander, Ruby Dee weeps, the window, raining, she calls,
and her voice
is left to hurt us slowly. It hangs against the same wet
glass, her
sadness and age, and the trip, and the lost heat, and the
grey cold
buildings of our entrapment. Ladies. Women. We need
you. We are still
trapped and weak, but we build and grow heavy with
our knowledge. Women.
Come to us. Help us get back what was always ours.
Help us. women. Where
are you, women, where, and who, and where, and who,
and will you help
us, will you open your bodysouls, will you lift me up
mother, will you
let me help you, daughter, wife/lover, will you

Babylon Revisited

The gaunt thing
with no organs
creeps along the streets
of Europe, she will
commute, in her feathered bat stomach-gown

with no organs
with sores on her insides
even her head
a vast puschamber
of pus(sy) memories
with no organs
nothing to make babies
she will be the great witch of euro-american legend
who sucked the life
from some unknown nigger
whose name will be known
but whose substance will not ever
not even by him
who is dead in a pile of dopeskin

This bitch killed a friend of mine named Bob Thompson
a black painter, a giant, once, she reduced
to a pitiful imitation faggot
full of American holes and a monkey on his back
slapped airplanes
from the empire state building

May this bitch and her sisters, all of them,
receive my words
in all their orifices like lye mixed with
cocola and alaga syrup

feel this shit, bitches, feel it, now laugh your
hysterectic laughs
while your flesh burns
and your eyes peel to red mud

leroy

I wanted to know my mother when she sat
looking sad across the campus in the late 20's
into the future of the soul, there were black angels
straining above her head, carrying life from our ancestors,
and knowledge, and the strong nigger feeling. She sat

(in that photo in the yearbook I showed Vashti) getting
  into
new blues, from the old ones, the trips and passions
showered on her by her own. Hypnotizing me, from so
  far
ago, from that vantage of knowledge passed on to her
  passed on
to me and all the other black people of our time.
When I die, the consciousness I carry I will to
black people. May they pick me apart and take the
useful parts, the sweet meat of my feelings. And leave
the bitter bullshit rotten white parts
alone.

A Poem Some People Will Have to Understand

Dull unwashed windows of eyes
and buildings of industry. What
industry do I practice? A slick
colored boy, 12 miles from his
home. I practice no industry.
I am no longer a credit
to my race. I read a little,
scratch against silence slow spring
afternoons.
        I had thought, before, some years ago
that I'd come to the end of my life.
        Watercolor ego. Without the preciseness
a violent man could propose.
        But the wheel, and the wheels,
wont let us alone. All the fantasy
        and justice, and dry charcoal winters
All the pitifully intelligent citizens
        I've forced myself to love.

        We have awaited the coming of a natural
        phenomenon. Mystics and romantics, knowledgeable
        workers
        of the land.

But none has come.
(*Repeat*)
            but none has come.

Will the machinegunners please step forward?

Letter To E. Franklin Frazier

Those days when it was all right
to be a criminal, or die, a postman's son,
full of hallways and garbage, behind the hotdog store
or in the parking lots of the beautiful beer factory.

Those days I rose through the smoke of chilling Satur-
    days
hiding my eyes from the shine boys, my mouth and my
    flesh
from their sisters. I walked quickly and always alone
watching the cheap city like I thought it would swell
and explode, and only my crooked breath could put it
    together
again.

By the projects and small banks of my time. Counting
    my steps
on tar or new pavement, following the sun like a park. I
    imagined
a life, that was realer than speech, or the city's anony-
    mous
fish markets. Shuddering at dusk, with a mile or so up
    the hill

to get home. Who did you love
then, Mussolini? What were you thinking,
Lady Day? A literal riddle of image
was me, and my smell was a continent
of familiar poetry. Walking the long way,
always the long way, and up the steep hill.

Those days like one drawn-out song, monotonously
promising. The quick step, the watchful march march,
All were leading here, to this room, where memory
stifles the present. And the future, my man, is long
time gone.

Numbers, Letters

If you're not home, where
are you? Where'd you go? What
were you doing when gone? When
you come back, better make it good.
What was you doing down there, freakin' off
with white women, hangin' out
with Queens, say it straight to be
understood straight, put it flat and real
in the street where the sun comes and the
moon comes and the cold wind in winter
waters your eyes. Say what you mean, dig
it out put it down, and be strong
about it.

I cant say who I am
unless you agree I'm real

I cant be anything I'm not
Except these words pretend
to life not yet explained,
so here's some feeling for you
see how you like it, what it
reveals, and that's me.

Unless you agree I'm real
that I can feel
whatever beats hardest
at our black souls

I am real, and I can't say who
I am. Ask me if I know, I'll say
yes, I might say no. Still, ask.

I'm Everett LeRoi Jones, 30 yrs old.
A black nigger in the universe. A long breath singer,
wouldbe dancer, strong from years of fantasy
and study. All this time then, for what's happening
now. All that spilling of white ether, clocks in ghostheads
lips drying and rewet, eyes opening and shut, mouths
    churning.

I am a meditative man. And when I say something it's
    all of me
saying, and all the things that make me, have formed me,
    colored me
this brilliant reddish night. I will say nothing that I feel
    is
lie, or unproven by the same ghostclocks, by the same
    riders
always move so fast with the word slung over their backs
    or
in saddlebags, charging down Chinese roads. I carry some
    words,
some feeling, some life in me. My heart is large as my
    mind
this is a messenger calling, over here, over here, open
    your eyes
and your ears and your souls; today is the history we
    must learn
to desire. There is no guilt in love

Young Soul

First, feel, then feel, then
read, or read, then feel, then
fall, or stand, where you
already are. Think
of your self, and the other
selves . . . think
of your parents, your mothers
and sisters, your bentslick
father, then feel, or
fall, on your knees
if nothing else will move you,

                then read
                and look deeply
                into all matters
                come close to you
                city boys—
                country men

                Make some muscle
                in your head, but
                use the muscle
                in yr heart

Cold Term

All the things. The objects.
Cold freeze of the park, while
passing. People there. White inside
outside on horses trotting ignorantly
There is so much pain for our blackness
so much beauty there, if we think to what
our beautiful selves would make
of the world, steaming turning blackouts
over cold georgia, the spirits hover
waiting for the world to arrive at ecstasy.
Why cant we love each other and be beautiful?

Why do the beautiful corner each other and spit
poison? Why do the beautiful not hangout together
and learn to do away with evil? Why are the beautiful
not living together and feeling each other's trials?
Why are the beautiful not walking with their arms around
each other laughing softly at the soft laughter of black
    beauty?
Why are the beautiful dreading each other, and hiding
    from
each other? Why are the beautiful sick and divided
like myself?

In one battle

Three grey boys tracked us to an old house.
We saw them coming winding collecting the weather
in their slow movement. Grey also their day
which is their faces, and their understanding
of where we are.

Our murderous intentions
are what they hear, and think them thin whore hawks
brushing through the trees.

The other guys are already aiming
as greys snake towards the house.
I take a few seconds, to finish
these notes, now my fingers eagerly
toward the machine

Return of the Native

Harlem is vicious
modernism. BangClash.
Vicious the way it's made.
Can you stand such beauty?
So violent and transforming.
The trees blink naked, being
so few. The women stare
and are in love with them
selves. The sky sits awake
over us. Screaming
at us. No rain.
Sun, hot cleaning sun
drives us under it.

The place, and place
meant of
black people. Their heavy Egypt.
(Weird word!) Their minds, mine,
the black hope mine. In Time.
We slide along in pain or too
happy. So much love
for us. All over, so much of
what we need. Can you sing
yourself, your life, your place
on the warm planet earth.
And look at the stones

the hearts, the gentle hum
of meaning. Each thing, life
we have, or love, is meant
for us in a world like this.
Where we may see ourselves
all the time. And suffer
in joy, that our lives
are so familiar.

Black Bourgeoisie,

has a gold tooth, sits long hours
on a stool thinking about money.
sees white skin in a secret room
rummages his sense for sense
dreams about Lincoln(s)
conks his daughter's hair
sends his coon to school
works very hard
grins politely in restaurants
has a good word to say
never says it
does not hate ofays
hates, instead, him self
him black self

Black Art

Poems are bullshit unless they are
teeth or trees or lemons piled
on a step. Or black ladies dying
of men leaving nickel hearts
beating them down. Fuck poems
and they are useful, wd they shoot
come at you, love what you are,
breathe like wrestlers, or shudder
strangely after pissing. We want live
words of the hip world live flesh &
coursing blood. Hearts Brains
Souls splintering fire. We want poems
like fists beating niggers out of Jocks
or dagger poems in the slimy bellies
of the owner-jews. Black poems to
smear on girlmamma mulatto bitches
whose brains are red jelly stuck
between 'lizabeth taylor's toes. Stinking
Whores! We want "poems that kill."

Assassin poems, Poems that shoot
guns. Poems that wrestle cops into alleys
and take their weapons leaving them dead
with tongues pulled out and sent to Ireland. Knockoff
poems for dope selling wops or slick halfwhite
politicians Airplane poems, rrrrrrrrrrrrrrrrr
rrrrrrrrrrrrrrr . . . tuhtuhtuhtuhtuhtuhtuhtuhtuh
. . . rrrrrrrrrrrrrrrrr . . . Setting fire and death to
whities ass. Look at the Liberal
Spokesman for the jews clutch his throat
& puke himself into eternity . . . rrrrrrrr
There's a negroleader pinned to
a bar stool in Sardi's eyeballs melting
in hot flame Another negroleader
on the steps of the white house one
kneeling between the sheriff's thighs
negotiating cooly for his people.
Agggh . . . stumbles across the room . . .
Put it on him, poem. Strip him naked
to the world! Another bad poem cracking
steel knuckles in a jewlady's mouth
Poem scream poison gas on beasts in green berets
Clean out the world for virtue and love,
Let there be no love poems written
until love can exist freely and
cleanly. Let Black People understand
that they are the lovers and the sons
of lovers and warriors and sons
of warriors Are poems & poets &
all the loveliness here in the world

We want a black poem. And a
Black World.
Let the world be a Black Poem
And Let All Black People Speak This Poem
Silently
or LOUD

Poem for Half White College Students

Who are you, listening to me, who are you
listening to yourself? Are you white or
black, or does that have anything to do
with it? Can you pop your fingers to no
music, except those wild monkies go on
in your head, can you jerk, to no melody,
except finger poppers get it together
when you turn from starchecking to checking
yourself. How do you sound, your words, are they
yours? The ghost you see in the mirror, is it really
you, can you swear you are not an imitation greyboy,
can you look right next to you in that chair, and swear,
that the sister you have your hand on is not really
so full of Elizabeth Taylor, Richard Burton is
coming out of her ears. You may even have to be Richard
with a white shirt and face, and four million negroes
think you cute, you may have to be Elizabeth Taylor, old
    lady,
if you want to sit up in your crazy spot dreaming about
    dresses,
and the sway of certain porters' hips. Check yourself,
    learn who it is
speaking, when you make some ultrasophisticated point,
    check yourself,
when you find yourself gesturing like Steve McQueen,
    check it out, ask
in your black heart who it is you are, and is that image
    black or white,

you might be surprised right out the window, whistling
    dixie on the way in

Black People!

What about that bad short you saw last week
on Frelinghuysen, or those stoves and refrigerators,
record players
in Sears, Bambergers, Klein's, Hahnes', Chase, and the
smaller joosh
enterprises? What about that bad jewelry, on Washing-
ton Street, and
those couple of shops on Springfield? You know how to
get it, you can
get it, no money down, no money never, money dont
grow on trees no
way, only whitey's got it, makes it with a machine, to
control you
you cant steal nothin from a white man, he's already stole
it he owes
you anything you want, even his life. All the stores will
open if you
will say the magic words. The magic words are: Up
against the wall mother
fucker this is a stick up! Or: Smash the window at night
(these are magic
actions) smash the windows daytime, anytime, together,
let's smash the
window drag the shit from in there. No money down.
No time to pay. Just
take what you want. The magic dance in the street. Run
up and down Broad
Street niggers, take the shit you want. Take their lives if
need be, but
get what you want what you need. Dance up and down
the streets, turn all
the music up, run through the streets with music, beauti-
ful radios on
Market Street, they are brought here especially for you.
Our brothers
are moving all over, smashing at jellywhite faces. We
must make our own

World, man, our own world, and we can not do this
    unless the white man
is dead. Let's get together and killhim my man, let's get
    to gather the fruit
of the sun, let's make a world we want black children to
    grow and learn in
do not let your children when they grow look in your
    face and curse you by
pitying your tomish ways.

A. B. SPELLMAN (1934–   )

When Black People Are

when black people are
with each other
we sometimes fear ourselves
whisper over our shoulders
about unmentionable acts
& sometimes we fight & lie.
these are somethings we sometimes do.

& when alone i sometimes walk
from wall to wall fighting visions
of white men fighting me
& black men fighting white men
& fighting me & i lose my
self between walls &
ricocheting shots & can't say
for certain who i have killed
or been killed by.

it is the fear of winter passing
& summer coming & the killing
i have called for coming
to my door saying
hit it a.b., you're in it too.

& the white army moves like thieves
in the night mass producing beautiful
black corpses & then stealing them away
while my frequent death watches me
from orangeburg on cronkite &
i'm oiling my gun & cooking my food
& saying "when the time comes"
to myself, over & over, hopefully.

but i remember driving from atlanta
to the city with stone & featherstone
& cleve & on the way feather talked
about ambushing a pair of klansmen
& cleve told how they hunted
chaney's body in the white night
of the haunted house in the Mississippi
swamp while a runaway survivor
from orangeburg slept between wars
on the back seat.
times like this
are times when black people
arc with cach other & the strength flows
back & forth between us like
borrowed breath.

In Orangeburg My Brothers Did

in orangeburg my brothers did
the african twist around a bonfire they'd built
at the gate to keep the hunkies out. the day
before they'd caught one shooting up
the campus like the white hunter
he was. but a bonfire? only conjures
up the devil. up popped the devil from behind a bush
the brothers danced the fire
danced the bullets cut their flesh
like bullets. black death
black death black death black
brothers black sisters black me with no white blood on
    my hands
we are so beautiful
we study our history backwards
& that must be the beast's most fatal message
that we die to learn it well.

JOHARI AMINI (1935–   )

Saint Malcolm

the prophet speaks
his images disseminate
    stripping facade
        and the Dream stands naked
            visibly before creation
        as the Nightmare
        in a truth of beasts grasping men

Prophecy is silenced of necessity
as nightmares erupt in fulfillment
    El Hajj Malik El Shabazz martyrized

But his word cauterizes our infection
unifying blackness

Utopia

brothers

brothers
everywhere—
    and
not a one
    for sale.

SONIA SANCHEZ (1935–   )

to all brothers

yeah.
        they
hang you up
those grey chicks
parading their
tight asses
in front of you.
some will say out
right
        baby i want
        to ball you
while smoother
ones will in
tegrate your
blackness
          yeah.
          brother
this sister knows
          and waits.

poem at thirty

it is midnight
no magical bewitching
hour for me
i know only that
i am here waiting
remembering that
once as a child
i walked two
miles in my sleep.

did i know
then where i
was going?
traveling. i'm
always traveling.
i want to tell
you about me
about nights on a
brown couch when
i wrapped my
bones in lint and
refused to move.
no one touches
me anymore.
father do not
send me out
among strangers.
you you black man
stretching scraping
the mold from your body.
here is my hand.
i am not afraid
of the night.

nigger

nigger.
        that word
ain't shit to me
man.
    don't u know
where u at when
u call me nigger?
look.
        my man. i'll
say it slow for you.
                N-I-G-G-E-R-

that word don't turn
me on man.
                    i know i am
black.
  -         beautiful.
                    with meaning.
nigger. u say.
                    my man
you   way behind the set

black magic

        magic
                    my man
        is you
                    turning
        my body into
        a thousand
        smiles.
                    black
        magic is your
        touch
                    making
        me breathe.

summary

no sleep tonight
not even after all
the red and green pills
i have pumped into
my stuttering self or
the sweet wine
that drowns them.
                    this is
a poem for the world
for the slow suicides

in seclusion.
somewhere on 130th st.
a woman, frail as a
child's ghost, sings.

            oh.
            oh. what
can the matter be? johnny's
so long at the fair.
          /i learned how
            to masturbate
thru the new york times.
i thought
shd i have
thought anything
that cd not
be proved. i
thought and
was wrong. listen.

               fool
       black
         bitch
of fantasy. life
is no more than
         gents
          and
            gigolos
            (99% american)
     liars
       and
    killers (199% american) dreamers
        and drunks (299%
            american)
(only god is 300% american)
              i say
is everybody happy?
this is a poem for me.
i am alone.
one night of words
will not change
all that.

LISTENEN TO BIG BLACK AT S.F. STATE

no mo meetings
where u talk bout
whitey. the cracker
who done u wrong
               (like some sad/bitch
who split in the middle of yo/comen)
just.   gitting.   stronNNNger.
                       maken warriors
outa boys.
        blk/woooomen
              outa girls.
                  moven in &
out of blkness
        till it runs this
              400/yr/old/road/show
(called
      amurica.
         now liven off its re/runs.)
                  off the road.
no mo tellen the man he is
            a dead/die/en/motha/
fucka.
     just a sound of drums.
              the sonnnnnNNg of chiefs
pouren outa our blk/sections.
      aree-um-doo-doo-doooooo-WORK
      aree-um-doo-doo-doooooo-LOVE
      arem-doooo-UNITY
      arem-doooo-LAND
      arem-doooo-WAR
      arem-doooo-BUILDEN

aree-um-doo-doo-dooooo.   MalcolMmmm
aree-um-doo-doo-dooooo.   ElijahHHH
aree-um-doo-doo-dooooo.   Imamuuuu

    just the sonnnng of chiefs.
      loud with blk/nation/hood
             builden.

a poem for my father

how sad it must be
to love so many women
to need so many black
perfumed bodies weeping
underneath you.

                        when i remember all those nights
i filled my mind with
long wars between short
sighted trojans & greeks
while you slapped some
wide hips about in
your pvt dungeon,
when i remember your
deformity   i want to
do something about your
makeshift manhood.
i guess
       that is why
on meeting your sixth
wife, i cross myself
with her confessionals.

hospital/poem

(for etheridge. 9/26/69)

they have sed
u will die in
this nite room
of tubes/
        red/death/screams.
                how do
they ima
       gine death?
            becuz yo/body

stops its earth
                movements
                            does not
mean it dies.
            blk/
                    mass can
not die maaan.   it regroups
                            to move
in to   another
                space.   a
                                nother time.
it is mor/ning
            maaaan.   still u do not
move
        and yo/hrs
                    slide into days
            and i watch u
                            as i
begin to talk
            of HYenaaaAAS.

summer words of a sistuh addict

the first day i shot dope
was on a sunday.
                    I had just come
home from church
                    got mad at my motha
cuz she got mad at me.   u dig?
                            went out.   shot up
behind a feelen gainst her.
                            it felt good.
gooder than dooing it.   yeah.
                            it was nice.
i did it.   uh.huh.   i did it.   uh. huh.

i want to do it again.   it felt so gooooood.
                                  and as the sistuh
                                  sits in her silent/
                                  remembered/high
                                  someone leans for
                                  ward gently asks her:
                                       sistuh.
                                       did u
                                       finally
                                  learn how to hold yo/mother?
and the music of the day
                          drifts in the room
to mingle with the sistuh's young tears.
              and we all sing.

                        —answer to yo/question
                         of am i not yo/woman
                         even if u went on shit again—

& i a beginner
                   in yo/love
say no.
        i wud not be yo/woman
& see u disappear
                        each day
befo my eyes
                and know yo/
reappearance
            to be
                  a one/
                        nite / stand.
no man.
        blk/
        lovers   cannot   live
in wite powder that removes
them from they blk/selves
                          cannot ride
majestic   /   wite   /   horses
                          in a machine age.

blk . /   lovers
                    must live   /
                              push against the
devils of this world
                    against the creeping
witeness of they own minds.
i am yo /   woman
                    my man.
                              and blk/women
deal in babies and
                    sweet / blk / kisses
and nites that
                    multiply by twos.

                    poem for etheridge

stone/
      cold/
            daylight   /.
                              moven
stretchen   turnen   togetha.
            changen
                    positions.
                              man.
this is fo real.
                    i am swingen/
                              man
      runnen/
                man
hangen upside down/
                    man.
      it   is   u
      it   is   u
      it   is   u
      it   is   u   /   my man.
ooowaheh—heh
ooowaheh—heh
                    ooooowaaawaaaheh—heh
                    ooooowaaawaaaheh—heh

music in my legs/
stomach
travelen to meet u man.
feel my
african   /   pulse rite now.
it is dark/
and beautifullee wet
pushen us
toward past   /   beginnings.
centuries passing
as we
dance our
togetha songs.
ahhhh beautiful
music
coveren our   blue   /   indigo   /
bodies . . . .

a chant for young   /   brothas
& sistuhs

yall

out there.   looooken so coool

in yo   /   highs.

yeah yall

rat there

listen to me

screeaamen this song.

did u know i've

seen yo / high

                             on every blk / st in

wite / amurica

                     i've seen yo/self/

imposed/quarantined/hipness

                                 on every

slum/

       bar/   revolutionary / st

& there yall be sitten.

                         u brotha.

u sisthu.

         listen to this drummen.

this sad / chant.

                   listen to the tears

flowen down my blk / face

                             listen to a

death/song being sung on thick/lips

by a blk/woman

              once i had a maaan
              who loved me so he sed
              we lived togetha, loved togetha
              and i followed wherever he led

now this maaan of mine
got tired of this slooow pace
started gitten high a lot
to stay on top of the race.

saw him begin to die
screeaamed. held him so tight
but he got so thin so very thin
slipped thru these fingers of might.

last time i heard from him
he was bangen on a woman's door
callen for his daily high
didn't even care bout the score.

once i loooved a man
still do looove that man
want to looove that man again
wish he'd come on home again

need to be with that maaannn
need to love that maaaannnn
who went out one day & died
who went out one day & died.

yall

    out there   looooken so cooool

in yo / highs.

        yeah.   yall

                rat there

c'mon down from yo / wite / highs

   and live.

JUNE JORDAN (1936–   )

Okay "Negroes"

Okay "Negroes"
American Negroes
looking for milk
crying out loud
in the nursery of freedomland:
the rides are rough.
Tell me where you got that image
of a male white mammy.
God is vague and he don't take no sides.
You think clean fingernails crossed legs a smile
shined shoes
a crucifix around your neck
good manners
no more noise
you think who's gonna give you something?

Come a little closer.
Where you from?

Cameo No. II

The name of this poem is

George Washington
somebody want me to think he bad

he bad

George Washington the father of this country
the most the first the roly-poly ghost
the father of this country
took my mother

anyway you want to take that

George the father full of rat fat
crazy hypocrite
his life some other bit
than freedom down to every man

George Washington he think he big
he trade my father for a pig

ignoble knave his ordinary
extraordinary human
slaves 300 people Black
and bleeding life beholden to the Presidential
owner underneath the powder of his wicked wig
he think he big

he pulled a blackman from his pocket
put a pig inside the other one
George Washington

the father of this country
stocked
by declarations at the auction block

Prez Washington he say
"give me niggers
let me pay

by check"
(Check the father of this country
what he say:)

"I always pay for niggers
let them stay
like vermin
at Mount Vernon"

impeccable in battle
ManKill Number One

the revolutionary head
aristocratic raider at the vulnerable
slavegirl bed

Americanus Rex
Secretus Blanco-Bronco-Night-Time-Sex

the father of this country
leading privileges of rape and run

George Washington

somebody tell me how he bad he big

I know how he
the great great great great
great great proto-

typical

**Poem for my family: Hazel Griffin
and Victor Hernandez Cruz**

Dedicated to Robert Penn Warren

I

December 15, 1811
a black, well-butchered slave
named George took leave of Old Kentucky—True
he left that living hell in pieces—
first his feet fell to the fire
and the jelly of his eyes lay smoking
on the pyre a long while—
but he burned complete
at last he left at least he got away
the others had to stay there

where he died like meat
(that slave)

how did he live?

December 15, 1811

Lilburn Lewis and his brother
cut and killed somebody real
because they missed their mother:
Thomas Jefferson's sweet sister Lucy
Correction: Killed no body: killed a slave
the time was close to Christmas sent the poor
black bastard to the snow zones of a blue-eyed
heaven and he went the way he came like meat
not good enough to eat
not nice enough to see
not light enough to live
he came the way he went like meat.

POEM FOR 175 Pounds
("Poor George")

II

Southern Kentucky, Memphis, New Orleans,
Little Rock, Milwaukee, Brooklyn, San Antonio,
Chicago
I am screaming
do you see the pulse
destroying properties
of your defense against me and my life
now what are you counting

dollar bills or lives?

How did you put me down
as property?
as life?
How did you describe the damage?
I am naked
I am Harlem and Detroit
currently knives and bullets
I am lives
YOUR PROPERTY IS DYING

I am lives
MY LIFE IS BEING BORN
This is a lesson
in American History
What can you teach me?
The fire smells of slavery.

III

Here is my voice the speed and the wondering
darkness of my desire is
all that I am here
all that you never allowed:
I came and went like meat not good enough to eat
remember no remember
yes remember me
the shadow following your dreams
the human sound that never reached your ears
that disappear
vestigial
when the question is my scream
and I am screaming
whiteman
do you hear the loud
the blood, the real hysteria of birth
my life is being born
your property is dying

IV

What can you seize
from the furnace
what can you save?
America
I mean America how
do you intend to incinerate
my slavery?
I have taken my eyes from the light of your fires.
The begging body grows cold.
I see.

I see my self
Alive
A life

Poem from the Empire State

Three of us went to the top of the city
a friend, my son, and I
on that day when winter wrote like snow
across the moonlike sky
and stood there breathing a heavy height
as wide as the streets to see
so poor and frozen far below
that nothing would change for you and me
that swallowing death lay wallowing still
with the wind at the bloat of piled-up swill
And that was the day we conquered the air
with 100,000 tons of garbage.

No rhyme can be said.
where reason has fled.

My Sadness Sits Around Me

My sadness sits around me
        not on haunches not in any
        placement near a move
and the tired roll-on
of a boredom without grief

If there were war
I would watch the hunting
I would chase the dogs
and blow the horn
because blood is commonplace

As I walk in peace
        unencountered unmolested
        unimpinging unbelieving unrevealing
        undesired under every O
My sadness sits around me

Nobody Riding the Roads Today

Nobody riding the roads today
But I hear the living rush
far away from my heart
Nobody meeting on the streets
But I rage from the crowded
overtones of emptiness

Nobody sleeping in my bed
but I breathe like windows
broken by emergencies

Nobody laughing anymore
But I see the world split
and twisted up like open stone

Nobody riding the roads today
But I hear the living rush
far away from my heart

What Happens

What happens when the dog sits on a tiger
when the fat man sells a picture of himself
when a lady shoves a sword inside her
when an elephant takes tea cups from the shelf

or the giant starts to cry
and the grizzly loses his grip
or the acrobat begins to fly
and gorillas run away with the whip

What happens when a boy sits on a chair
and watches all the action on the ground and
in the air
or when the children leave the greatest
show on earth
and see the circus?

LUCILLE CLIFTON (1936–   )

Good times

My Daddy has paid the rent
and the insurance man is gone
and the lights is back on
and my uncle Brud has hit
for one dollar straight
and they is good times
good times
good times

My Mama has made bread
and Grampaw has come
and everybody is drunk
and dancing in the kitchen
and singing in the kitchen
oh these is good times
good times
good times

oh children think about the
good times

Love Rejected

Love rejected
hurts so much more
than Love rejecting;
they act like they don't love their country
No
what it is
is they found out
their country don't love them.

Admonitions

boys
i don't promise you nothing
but this
what you pawn
i will redeem
what you steal
i will conceal
my private silence to
your public guilt
is all i got

girls
first time a white man
opens his fly
like a good thing
we'll just laugh
laugh real loud my
black women

children
when they ask you
why is your mama so funny
say
she is a poet
she don't have no sense

If I Stand in My Window

If I stand in my window
naked in my own house
and press my breasts
against my windowpane
like black birds pushing against glass
because I am somebody
in a New Thing

and if the man come to stop me
in my own house
naked in my own window
saying I have offended him
I have offended his

Gods

let him watch my black body
push against my own glass
let him discover self
let him run naked through the streets
crying
praying in tongues

JAMES W. THOMPSON (1936–   )

A Constant Labor

my light will tip tankards of fire in the sky—
    burning old despairing roots.
    and I, I dare extol the sun
    extract remembrances begun
    at evenings projectile edge;
    in the pulsating mouth of midnights
    as worms churn in the skull,
    and time carves tempests on the soul and sinew.

I will chorus the rise of fear, and fall of foe:
    the slow fusing of feeling into form,
    radiating with the wind and whispering
    of wings and leaves on abrupt abandoned piers;
    of spires of moonlight puncturing hopeful faces
    and the thousand minute traces
    of the last frost's fecund seeping,
    and the distant sound of creepings from vapid wells.

I will recede, from moist thighs of certain felt delights
    as melting winter before the spring—
    dazzling and drained—only to enter again
    the several sensual scents, and sights,
    ever tumbling heights and rumbling sighs of life:
    the fertile midnight, straining
    in the lavish bed of morning.

The Greek Room

what was it
that caught in our throats that day,
like bits of sweet apple
choking our voices,
pregnant for want of a language—
a carpet of words to spread before us?

what compulsion captured them
in that expectant state,
tossed them abstracts of images
to create our speech?

we conversed in shaded tones
painting shadows without substance,
composing distorted pictures of ourselves
for what seemed the other's delight
till we grew weary, and said goodnight.

to our separate dismay
at each encounter thereafter,
we built a greek room of marble figures
to enclose our love; a flame untouched by fire
spreading sparklets in a spiral glow of light,
cold as diamond.

The spawn of slums

To a Negro Writer

I was never the light lad
on the long road over
happy heights and hollows
in the haughty young sun.

At birth I was knighted,
and in vassalage blighted;

crammed in a dank tomb
in the camp of the dungeoned.

The sun refused to bloom
and most minds were bludgeoned;
Still laughter lifted listless day's drowning,
in a enveloping filigree bright as mail.

And the intricate harmonies became a grail
to steady the stumbling at the lighting
of frayed fringe, pipe thin, lamps.
Yes—there's ferment in the camps.

The lassitude the limits
of the camp imposed: on hands
whose knowing kneading
pampered or punished me;

On lips whose petulant
postures popped, painting
mists and mountains on
my cheeks and brow

was not then known to me
—but they are now—
And I was never
at a loss for love.

Still—I never asked a thing of dawn,
forging venomous verdicts
I left them to spawn
in a crypt of heart,

violent in beating
each sacred part
laced with lashings not received
by me—but to be relieved

by my being born
to break the blight
and blast the bastard jackals
lapping at my mother's heels.

The Plight

(theme variation fugue & coda movement)

It is the silver seeking salvation
that strains between the garland gaiety
of the backyard fence where bells
and berries, roses & rhododendrums
wrestle weeds in the sinking light.

The sinking silver slays
rhododendrum's rose, the bell's berry;
twisting, their shrinking skeletons
strangle the fence in shifting shadows,
swallowed in weeds—the silver sunk.

> The moon is silver
> the moon is cold
> the moon is sterile
> the moon is old

> The sun is sienna, gold enlaid
> the sun is master, mother, maid
> the sun is strength
> the sun is song

> AND THE MOON IS SHORT
> BUT THE SUN IS LONG

Salvation was the silver god
commanding the rhododendrum & the rose,
the bells and the berries, to green
and brown in the garish compound—
forging a futile future for flowers.

Flowers feigned the forgery
fogging salvations silver view
bells berries & rhododendrums rose,
saved by silver-god's salvation—
freed by the facility of fences.

God is salvation
God's the staff
God is good
God's the shaft

Flower is fragrance
flower is free
flower is fruit
flower's me

AND GODS ARE SUPPOSED
BUT FLOWERS BE

JOHN RAVEN (1936–)

An Inconvenience

Mama,
papa,
and us
10 kids
lived in
a single room.
Once, when I
got sick
and like to die,
I heard a cry
slice through the gloom
"Hotdog!
We gon have
mo room!"

6/16/69

Assailant

He jumped me while I was asleep.
He was big and fat.
I been in many fights before,
but never one like that.
The only way I could survive,
was to get my hat . . .
His *name?*
Officers, I ain't talkin' 'bout no man;
I'm talkin' 'bout a rat!

4/9/69

The Roach

A roach
came struttin
across my bedroom
floor,
like it was beyond
reproach,
or was
some sexy-lookin
whore,
and if I hadn't
snuffed it,
left it
alive,
I know it would've
come right up
and gave me
five!

CAROLYN M. RODGERS

Now Ain't That Love?

who would
who could
      understand that
when i'm near him
i am a skinny, dumb, knock-kneed
lackey, drooling on the words of
my maharajah (or what/ever they call them
                  in those jive textbooks)

me. i am a bitch. hot.
panting for a pat from his hand
so i can wag my
love in front of his
      face. a princess, black.
dopey with lust, waiting
for the kiss of action from my
      prince. now i know that this
whole scene is not
      cool, but it's real!
so a-live—dig it! sometimes we be so close
      i can cop his pulse
and think it's my heart that i
      hear
in my ears. uh. now ain't that love?

Testimony

God—
they fear you, they hold you so
tight they squeeze the truth in you
out, (you run wild in my soul). I
know you are not the whip they
dream of, you do not tell them to
scrape their hearts and knees, moaning
while whitey kicks pockets in their
asses, they make you a gauze puppet, a
dumb parrot for their whims and darky-time
whispers. You do not ask them to fornicate
with some preacher's chicken/funky feelings
who jingles coins and sisters drawers for
salvation and spasms.

If you are the soldier they shout you are
shoot! Shoot then jesus, shoot buckshot
in their hearts. Let them know that heaven
is a hole in the air and hell needs its
teeth kicked out, here and now!

One

People die from loneliness.
Life becomes an incurable disease,
a job, an excuse—an operation
of sloppy dissections.

There is a constipation of the
heart, a diarrhea of need. Be-
ing is instinct, the body a
machine—the mind a lever or

the body the lever, the mind the
machine; in either case, operating
and driving on. And skin tightening
up bone until you mouth at the misery

and bargain with the ache. This is
not to say I am giving up, even
though life has pumped me up with
the pain. The rules are there.

I am the stray one.

for h. w. fuller

a man, standing in the shadows of a
white marble building
chipping at the stones earnestly, tirelessly,
moving with the changes of the hours,
the days,
the seasons and years,
using the shadows to shield him
such a man,
can go un noticed . . .

a Black Man standing in the shadows
is not like the one who straggles
through open spaces, hurls bricks at
windows, shatters glass,
yanks or kicks the doors down and
beats his chest, scream/proclaiming his glory—
these ones are removed, swiftly.

but the man who grows inside the shadows,
chipping at the foundation, long after
windows and doors have been replaced,
the man, who becomes the dark shadow of a
white marble building, will
pick the foundation to pieces,
chip by chip, and

the
building
will
fall.

Breakthrough

I've had tangled feelings lately
            about ev'rything
bout writing poetry, and otha forms
bout talkin and dreamin with a
special man (who says he needs me)
            uh huh
and my mouth has been open
            most of the time, but
I ain't been saying nothin but
            thinking about ev'rything
and the partial pain has been
how do I put my self on paper
the way I want to be or am and be
not like any one else in this
Black world but me

how do I sing some lyrics ev'ry most could dig but
don't always be riffin like twenty ten othas
            ev'rybodi's faintly heard. the trouble
is I tell you, how can I
sound just like and only my self
            and then could you dig it if I could?

u see, the changes are so many
there are several of me and
            all of us fight to show up at the same time
and there is uh consistent incongruity
      do u for instance, understand
      what I mean when I say
                        I am very tired of and trying
and want Blackness which is my life, want this to be
easier on me, want it not to suck me in and
out so much leavin me a balloon with no air, want it
not to puff me up so much sometimes
that I git puffed up and sucked in   in   to the
raunchy kind of love Black orgy I go through. do
u dig what I mean when I say I want to scream
fuck it all some days and then want to cry when

I walk around the street with my hurt my mind and
and some miscellaneous littl brotha
who's ultimately playin with my feelins sayin
    "what's happenin beautiful Black sistuh?"
can u dig why I want to say to him
    "why should u care?" and "why would u make me
love and puff all over again and instead I end up
smilin and sayin, "U got it littl bro"
        because
I think he needs, and he thought I needed

                                and the
be cause is the why, and that kinda style goes on
and I become trite in my dreams
and my poems fidget and why should I care that I
can't sound as original as I think my thoughts are,
but can you dig how it could
make me question my thoughts?
    how did I ever get in this mess—
    is mess this, don't u ever sit around and want
    to get very high offa somethin and cry be cause
            u   are
and then what am I supposed to tell my self
when I want to take long bus rides and cop sunsets
for the soul I'm not sure I have/would want it, and
sometimes I want to hibernate in the summer
    and hang out in the winter and nurse babies
and get fat and lay around and be pinched by my man
and just love and laugh all the time, even if the
sun don't shine
                and then the kids go to marching and
singing songs talkin bout Blackness and schools that
ain't schools and I know what they be talkin bout
    they know that I know what needs doin and what
has all or any of this or that got to do with the
fact that I want to write a POEM, a poem poem, a
    poem's poem poem on a poem that ev'ry u could
dig, just if only a littl bit
in between, underneath, on top or a-round a word
or feelin
            and not mind the fact that it might

sound faintly like some riffin u heard,
or not mind that it's not like anything
u could have been told about to understand
    but like reading breathing or sipp-savorin uh mind
and uh hung over ecstasy in what is and ain't gon be
and uh stiff won't rub off don't wash out longing
    for what u never had and can't imagine how u could
long for it since u'r not even sure it is
anyhow, like u or I is and I really hope that
        if u read this u
        will dig where I'm at
        and feel what I mean/   that/   where
            i am
    and could very possibly
            be
            real
        at this lopsided crystal sweet moment . . .

What Color is Lonely

for Barbara

Since you wrote a poem
explaining
the color of Black—
and I know that I am Black
                    Blacker
                        and Blackless sometimes,

Tell me sister,
What color is lonely?

Is it/am I blue
when I been hearin the
Epics sing "Uh Very Sad Story"
ova & ova &
can't stand tuh hear it anymo—

Is it/am I red
when uh brotha half hits because
he's uh 150% player—

Is it/am I green
when I see two nappy heads
growin into each otha—

Is it/am I Black on Black
when I sit for hours that
trickle befo me like unfreezin water
& I write poems about Black Unity—

Since you wrote a poem explaining
the sweet changes we are as Blacks
and I know how various yet unchanging
Blackness is,

Tell me sister,
What color is lonely?

Yuh Lookin GOOD

Meetings meetings meetings
rooms crowded spaces
sweaty smoki rapping
and the brothas, the brothas
the oh so fine brothas
with the hair, the fuzz,
the nat'chal kinky hair
and the beards and goatees
and the rapping to us sisters
to each otha, can u dig it?
about us makin it,
as a people
as a nation
a Third World

and me sittin around diggin
that if the cause, the movement
don't make us sisters militant, (about somethin!)
the brothas, the beautiful brothas
sho will!

LARRY NEAL (1937–   )

Harlem Gallery: From the Inside

The bars on Eighth Avenue in Harlem
glow real yellow, hard against formica
tables; they speak of wandering ghosts
and Harlem saints; the words lay slick
on greasy floors: rain wet butt in the junkie's
mouth, damp notebook in the number-runner's hand.
no heads turn as the deal goes down—we wait.

The Harlem rain explodes, flooding the avenues
rats float up out of the sewers. Do we need the
Miracles or a miracle?

Listen baby, to the mean scar-faced sister,
between you and her and me and you there are no
distances. short reach of the .38, a sudden burning
in the breast, a huge migraine hammering where your
    brain
used to be. then it's over, no distance between the needle
and the rope. instant time, my man, history is one quick
fuck; you no sooner in then you come, a quick fuck.

uptight against the sound, but everything ain't all right.
nitty-gritty would-be warriors snap fingers, ghosts booga-
loo against the haze, Malcolm eyes in the yellow glow
blood on black hands. compacted rooms of gloom, Gar-
    vey's
flesh in the rat's teeth. Lady Day at 100 centre street,
Charlie Parker dying in the penthouse of an aristocratic
bitch. Carlos Cook, Ras, Shine, Langston, the Barefoot
Prophet. Ira Kemp, the Signifying Monkey, Bud Powell.
Trane, Prez, Chano Pozo, Eloise Moore—all
falling faces in the Harlem rain
asphalt memory of blood and pain.

James Powell on Imagination*

We sit watching the afternoon summer smell ripely,
and we talk adventure, forgetting that all of the
indians are dead, and that the cavalry is on the hill
ready to sound the charge on us. boy talk.

Summer girls flirt down our fantasies,
looking for imaginary john waynes whose law
is not a six-shooter but a zip-gun.

*Step back sally, sally, sally
jump back in the alley, alley, alley.*

and then there are nights, outdoor movies
for the neighbors, and you are a speedster
in the star-sky toward your own planet

*old king glory of the mountain
the mountain was so high
it nearly touched the sky
the first one, the second one,
the third follow me . . .*

Yes, follow me, all of the me's
through my boy-man changes
through summers
that end in my death as I learn about
policemen who shoot real bullets into real people.

Malcolm X—An Autobiography

I am the Seventh Son of the Son
who was also the Seventh.
I have drunk deep of the waters of my ancestors
have travelled the soul's journey towards cosmic har-
mony,

---

* Shot by Lt. Thomas Gilligan, summer of 1964.

the Seventh Son.
Have walked slick avenues
and seen grown men, fall, to die in a blue doom
of death and ancestral agony,
have seen old men glide, shadowless, feet barely
touching the pavements.

I sprung out of the Midwestern plains
the bleak Michigan landscape wearing the slave name—
Malcolm Little.
Saw a brief vision in Lansing when I was seven, and in
my mother's womb heard the beast cry of death,
a landscape on which white robed figures ride, and my
Garvey father silhouetted against the night-fire, gun in
    hand
form outlined against a panorama of violence.

Out of the midwestern bleakness, I sprang, pushed east-
    ward,
past shack on country nigger shack, across the wilderness
of North America.

I hustler. I pimp. I unfulfilled Black man
bursting with destiny.
New York city Slim called me Big Red,
and there was no escape, close nights of the smell of
    death.
Pimp. hustler. The day fills these rooms.
I am talking about New York. Harlem.
talking about the neon madness.
talking about ghetto eyes and nights
talking about death protruding across the room. Small's
    paradise.
talking about cigarette butts, and rooms smelly with
    white
sex flesh, and dank sheets, and being on the run.
talking about cocaine illusions, about stealing and sell-
    ing.
talking about these New York cops who smell of blood
    and money.

I am Big Red, tiger vicious, Big Red, bad nigger, will
    kill.

But there is rhythm here. Its own special substance:
I hear Billie sing, no good man, and dig Prez, wearing
    the Zoot
suit of life, the pork-pie hat tilted at the correct angle.
through the Harlem smoke of beer and whiskey, I un-
    derstand the
mystery of the signifying monkey,
in a blue haze of inspiration, I reach for the totality of
    Being.
I am at the center of a swirl of events. War and death.
rhythm. hot women. I think life a commodity bargained
    for
across the bar in Small's.
I perceive the echoes of Bird and there is a gnawing in
    the maw
of my emotions.

and then there is jail. America is the world's greatest
    jailer,
and we all in jails. Black spirits contained like magnifi-
    cent
birds of wonder. I now understand my father urged on
    by the
ghost of Garvey,
and see a small brown man standing in a corner. The
    cell. cold.
dank. The light around him vibrates. Am I crazy? But to
    under-
stand is to submit to a more perfect will, a more perfect
    order.
To understand is to surrender the imperfect self.
For a more perfect self.

Allah formed black man, I follow
and shake within the very depth of my most imperfect
    being,
and I bear witness to the Message of Allah
and I bear witness—all praise is due Allah!

JAMES A. RANDALL, JR. (1938–   )

Who Shall Die?

Walk out into your country.
Whose is it?
Not the "polack's" not the "fascist's" or the "immigrant's,"
Or the "nigger's" with his dreams bitten off.
It belongs to no one;
Those who profess to love it
Feel nothing in the quagmire of broken faces
Where reprehensible magnates step,
The cry of the smallest bird is buried
In 200 years of filth shit on:
So the human being, defiled, chokes
On the wrongness of his dream,
Is gorged with chrome, steel, and vomits up
The excrement of slums.
He who shall die, buried to his eyes
In the racist hegemony, in the backward-running
Movie called the rights of man,
He who shall die unlamented, part of the nation still,
Whatever the politicians promise
In this or that election year . . . Nothing happens.

    By a white stream, in a white dream,
    A white God with white ideas,
    White as a white dove whom no one will love,
    The dove of death.

"Large commercial investments required . . ."
"The ghetto is a sociological phenomenon . . ."
"They're better off as they are . . ."
Nothing happens.
The aspirations of nation, ethic.
What are these?
There is a nightwind,

There is a blowing
There is a bloodletting of the mind.
To the universally dispossessed,
There is
The sterilization of desire. In these
Such a wind is building,
Harsh by night, in a darkness
With no silence,
Cricket-words buried,

Those who are hated shall surely
Give hate in return,
Those who are despised shall despise equally.
But all the poets of the world's past,
Pushed on by dreams and great deeds,
Cannot match the beauty of one
Who sits alone
In a house someone else owns,
Who very carefully,
Who very slowly
Pulls out a long blade,
Who slit his throat . . .

Untitled

Why should I bc eaten by love,
Eaten alive?
One should strike out, become
A "self," touch life
At its centermost spot

I can't escape my colour, impossible
To hide for a second, a moment,
Something forces it. Today, yesterday
The word "nigger" is God, is
Jesus, a white patriarch brought
To the New World on the backs
Of slaves. Oh God!

If you exist anywhere, anytime,
In some small corner of this existence,
You should rise up,
You should make us men again,
For the first time
Eat us within your love.

There is too much
Sadness to bear with,
This 300 year poem
To our suffering. For you, you this atheist.

Don't Ask Me Who I Am

dont ask me who i am, i
wont tell you, cant
& dont put your goddamn con-
descending paws around
me for the sake of
"existential brotherhood"
no words mean, thats why . . .
no words mean standing on a corner
in another world
no words mean . . .
        (Someone falling
        to his heart in filth)
or become because i wont become
        (Rats rounding corners
        like locomotives)
what you think i am

the only open door
is the door to man

When Something Happens

Sometimes, when you're called a bastard
over a period, say,
of several centuries;
sometimes, when you've opened your brain
to a window in the sky,
become almost a bird for want
of flying;
sometimes, when a child walking
in your eyes is shot,
feeling, somehow, what you wish to forget,
through all cities your stark sorrow moving
where the sun leaks hideously
its garbage and the garbage
rots in your own stuffed room
and no one
in all the world gives a damn,
are firing rockets, are
ramming the roof of Heaven, are
crowning glory with glory . . .
Sometimes something happens

and happens and happens
when your breathing shape is tired to death
of being told
how well it lives,
how decent stinking ghetto,
the milk skimmed off to show, to demonstrate
this vegetable darkness.
When you are cheated, when
even netted fish find more freedom
and the eyes of stuffed beasts,
the eyes that never shut, seem
to mock you with their stuffed look—
you lead your blind family
from darkness to darkness,
on C Street on 5th Avenue look for work,
move your beast where

the white gods spit
and the El's grey slug sparks along tracks
and cattle are butchered far from farms
and farm boys wonder
who you are how so many millions
stand, shaded, different.

Let one word be spoken; let
the sky jump under your fists; let
the sun go out, drenched in your tears,
no leaf be still,
but the generations of trees transmuted
by your found anger; let
pushcarts lose their geometric rims,
the circles fall apart.
O God! Something
happens in this new world prison,
when prisoners rise up!

I think
the prairies are wildly waving.
I think
the zones are unbecoming.
I think
those divided cities are hovering in alliance;
in America, in America
as purified out of a final fire
you rise up, you continually elaborate
the tribal speech, the speech
of this Western tribe,
far from Africa, coming back, coming back
without the introvert bleating
about "origins."
You who will find your sleep
on a grass hill that is yours because you made it;
you, when the love has been worn out of you,
love still; on a flame hill,
the flame eating, give back a greater light,
who are, with the Indians,
the first Americans.

Execution

It's just no use,
trying to be like them.
One comes, a giant
With filmy surgeon's gloves,
to put out your life. Click!
"The switches are going
to be shut down, one by one.
Your kinky hair. Click!
Your black face. Click!
Your nose, eyes, skin . . . Click!"

In the anteroom, where
you've been waiting all your life,
the female of the species,
Carnivorous Destructi,
wheels by a steel cart piled with
human organs.
The rubber tires black the floor.
Electricity spills
from her blonde hair. The room
juggles, fades, reappears.
But it's no use, madam,
none of this will work.

That afternoon gloves returns,
to show you, to make you see, to plead.
There are large tears in his eyes.
Become, he says.
Join us. You are a dead race.
Nigger.

When? Perhaps never.
Perhaps it will never come,
falling down to wings,
a circling plummet to water.
Oh! the very last
beautiful, the body turning
and twisting in the maw of the sea.
Nigger.

"Come now, don't be
afraid, the doctor won't
the doctor won't
the doctor . . ."

In the cell your eyes
suck up the porridge of light.
The caucasian gods hover around you.
A mechanism descends.
You are outside yourself.
Because it is no longer possible
to be yourself,
you become no one.
You know it is possible to be mad.
You carry your head under your arms
The nurse spits on it.
The spittle bites:
Nigger!
Her butt is swaying under the white.

They take away the nothing that was yours.
Better to die, you think.
But nothing happens.

Jew

Where he stood and where
He leaned, all at one time,
The urge to convey, like
The yellow star, long since gone,
An indignant earth still banged at his feet,
Who had strode through history burning.
But to look at him,
The piercing stare tumbling off
Into incomprehensible italics,
One would think otherwise,
One would think that the will
To be free had never lodged
In his bones.

He looked old, worn.
In his eyes flashed a peculiar
Irony. When I dreamed,
I saw clearly the ironic messages
That were his eyes;
Just the meaningful smile,
The teeth curved by the lips.

Somewhere in the flesh mirror
I saw myself.
And after the silent promise,
I, feeling something heavier
Than the tortured face,
Felt the bewilderment of one
Who has recalled his murdering.

WELTON SMITH

malcolm

i cannot move
from your voice.
there is no peace
where i am. the wind
cannot move
hard enough to clear the trash
and far away i hear my screams.

the lean, hard-bone face
a rich copper color.
the smile. the
thin nose and broad
nostrils. Betty—in the quiet
after midnight. your hand
soft on her back. you kiss
her neck softly
below her right ear.
she would turn
to face you and arch up—
her head moving to your chest.
her arms sliding
round your neck. you breathe deeply.
it is quiet. in this moment
you know
what it was all about

your voice
is inside me; i loaned
my heart in exchange
for your voice.
in harlem, the long
avenue blocks. the miles
from heart to heart.

a slobbering emaciated man
once a man of god sprawled
on the sidewalk. he clutches
his bottle. pisses on himself
demands you respect him
because his great grandmother
was one-eighth cherokee.
in this moment, you knew.

in berkeley the fat
jewess moves the stringy brown
hair from her face saying
she would like to help you—
give you some of her time.
you knew.
in birmingham "get a move
on you, girl. you bet'not
be late for sunday school."
not this morning—
it is a design. you knew.

sometimes
light plays on my eyelashes
when my eyes
are almost closed—
the chrome blues and golds
the crimson and pale
ice green   the swift movements
of lights through my lashes—
fantastic—
the sound of mecca
inside you. you knew.

the man
inside you; the men
inside you fought.
fighting men inside you
made a frenzy
smelling like shit.
you reached into yourself—

deep—and scooped your frenzy
and rolled it to a slimy ball
and stretched your arm back
to throw

now you pace the regions
of my heart. you know
my blood and see
where my tears are made.

i see the beast
and hold my frenzy;
you are not lonely—
in my heart there are many
unmarked graves.

The Nigga Section

slimy obscene creatures. insane
creations of a beast. you
have murdered a man. you
have devoured me. you
have done it with precision
like the way you stand green
in the dark sucking pus
and slicing your penis
into quarters—stuffing
shit through your noses.
you rotten motherfuckin bastards
murder yourselves again and again
and call it life. you have made
your black mother to spread
her legs   wide
you have crawled in mucus
smeared snot in your hair
let machines crawl up your cock
rammed your penis into garbage disposals
spread your gigantic ass from

one end of america to the other
and peeped from under your legs
and grinned a gigantic white grin
and called all the beasts
to fuck you hard in the ass
you have fucked your fat black mothers
you have murdered malcolm
you have torn out your own tongue
you have made your women
to grow huge dicks you
have stuffed me into your mouth
and slobbered my blood
in your grinning derangement.
you are the dumbest thing
on the earth   the slimiest
most rotten thing in the universe
you motherfuckin germ
you konk-haired blood suckin punks
you serpents of pestilence you
samboes you green witches gnawing the heads of infants
you rodents you whores
you sodomites you fat
slimy cockroaches crawling to your
holes with bits of malcolm's flesh
i hope you are smothered
in the fall of a huge yellow moon.

ISHMAEL REED (1938–   )

badman of the guest professor

*for joe overstreet, david henderson, albert ayler &
d mysterious "H" who cut up d rembrandts*

1

you worry me whoever you are
i know you didn't want me to
come here but hère i am just
d same; hi-jacking yr stagecoach,
hauling in yr pocket watches & mak
ing you hoof it all d way to
town. black bart, a robber w/ an
art; i left some curses in d cash
box so youll know its me

listen man, i cant help it if
yr thing is over, kaputs,
        finis
no matter how you slice it dick
you are done. a dead duck all out
of quacks; d nagging hiccup dat
goes on & on w/ out a simple glass
        of water for relief

2

youve been teaching shakespeare for
20 years only to find d joke
        on you
d eavesdropping rascal who got it
in d shins because he didnt know
enough to keep his feet behind d cur
tains; a sad-sacked head served on a

platter in titus andronicus or falstaff
    too fat to make a go of it
    anymore

3

its not my fault dat yr tradition
was knocked off wop style & left in
d alley w/pricks in its mouth. i
read abt it in d papers but it was no
    skin off my nose
wasnt me who opened d gates & allowed
d rustlers to slip thru unnoticed. you
ought to do something abt yr security or
    mend yr fences partner
dont look at me if all dese niggers
are ripping it up like deadwood dick;
doing art d way its never been done, mak
ing wurlitzer sorry he made d piano dat
will drive mozart to d tennis
    courts
making smith-corona feel like d red
faced university dat has just delivered china
    some 50 e-leben h bomb experts

i didnt deliver d blow dat drove d
abstract expressionists to mi ladies
linoleum where dey sleep beneath tons of
wax & dogshit & d muddy feet of children or
because some badassed blackpainter done sent
french impressionism to d walls of highrise
    lobbies where dey belong is not my fault
martha graham will never do d jerk
shes a sweet ol soul but her hips
cant roll; as stiff as d greek
statues she loves so much

4

dese are d reasons you did me nasty
j alfred prufrock, d trick you pull

ed in d bookstore today; stand in d
corner no peaches for a week, u lemon

u must blame me because yr wife is
ugly. 86-d by a thousand discriminating
saunas. dats why you did dat sneaky thing
i wont tell d townsfolk because u hv
to live here and im just passing thru

5

you got one thing right tho. i did say
dat everytime i read william faulkner i
go to sleep. when i read hemmingway i
wish dat one of dem bulls wd hv jumped d
fence & gored his fingers so dat he wdnt hv
taken up so much
                    good space

fitzgerald wdnt hv known a gangster if one
had snatched zelda & made her a moll tho
        she wd hv been grateful i bet

bonnie of clyde wrote d saga of suicide
sal just as d feds were closing in. it is
worth more than d collected works of ts
eliot a trembling anglican whose address
is now d hell dat thrilled him so
last word from down there he was open
ing a publishing co dat will bore d
devil back to paradise

6

& by d way did you hear abt grammar?
cut to ribbons in a photo finish by
stevie wonder, a blindboy who dances
on a heel. he just came out of d slang
& broke it down before millions.
        it was bloody murder

7

to make a long poem shorter—3 things
     moleheaded lame w/ 4 or 5 eyes
1) yr world is riding off into d sunset
2) d chips are down & nobody will chance yr i.o.u.s
3) d last wish was a fluke so now you hv to return to be-
   ing a fish
p.s. d enchantment has worn off

dats why you didn't like my reading list   right?
it didn't include anyone on it dat you cd in
vite to a cocktail party & shoot a lot of
     bull   right?
so you want to take it out on my hide   right?
well i got news for you professor nothing—i
am my own brand while you must be d fantasy of
     a japanese cartoonist

a strangekind of dinosaurmouse
i can see it all now. d leaves
are running low. its d eve of
extinction & dere are no holes to
accept yr behind. you wander abt yr
long neck probing a tree. you think
its a tree but its really a trap. a
cry of victory goes up in d kitchen of
d world. a pest is dead. a prehis
toric pest at dat. really funnytime
prehistoric pest whom we will lug into
a museum to show everyone how really funny
you are   yr fate wd make a good
scenario but d plot is between you &
charles darwin. you know, whitefolkese
     business

as is said. im passing thru. just sing
ing my song. get along little doggie &
jazz like dat. word has it dat a big gold

shipment is coming to californy. i hv to
ride all night if im to meet my pardners
dey want me to help score d ambush

black power poem

a spectre is haunting america—the spectre of hoodooism .
all the powers of old america have entered into a holy
   alli
ance to exorcise this spectre : allen ginsberg timothy
   leary
richard nixon richard daley time magazine the new york
   review
of books and the underground press .
may the best church win .   shake hands now and come
out conjuring

Beware :   Do Not Read This Poem

tonite, thriller was
abt an ol woman, so vain she
surrounded herself w/
       many mirrors

it got so bad that finally she
locked herself indoors & her
whole life became the
       mirrors

one day the villagers broke
into her house , but she was too
swift for them . she disappeared
       into a mirror
each tenant who bought the house
after that , lost a loved one to

the ol woman in the mirror :
first a little girl
then a young woman
then the young woman/s husband

the hunger of this poem is legendary
it has taken in many victims
back off from this poem
it has drawn in yr feet
back off from this poem
it has drawn in yr legs

back off from this poem
it is a greedy mirror
you are into this poem . from
    the waist down
nobody can hear you can they ?
this poem has had you up to here
    belch
this poem aint got no manners
you cant call out frm this poem
relax now & go w/ this poem

move & roll on to this poem
do not resist this poem
this poem has yr eyes
this poem has his head
this poem has his arms
this poem has his fingers
this poem has his fingertips

this poem is the reader & the
reader this poem

statistic : the us bureau of missing persons re-
        ports that in 1968 over 100,000 people
        disappeared leaving no solid clues
            nor trace   only
    a space   in the lives of their friends

MICHAEL HARPER (1938–)

Elvin's Blues

(for Elvin Jones)

Sniffed, dilating my nostrils,
The cocaine creeps up my
leg, smacks into my groin;
Naked with a bone for luck,
I linger in stickiness,
Tickled in the joints;
I will always be high—

Tired of fresh air,
the stone ground bread,
the humid chant of music
which has led me here,
I reed my song:

"They called me the black
narcissus as I devoured
'the white hopes'
crippled in their inarticulate
madness,
Crippled myself,
Drums, each like porcelain
chamber pots, upside down,
I hear a faggot insult my
white wife with a sexless grin,
maggots under his eyelids,
a candle of my fistprint
breaks the membrane of his nose.
Now he stutters."

Last Thursday, I lay with you
tincturing your womb

with aimless strokes I could not feel.
Swollen and hard the weekend,
penitent, inane
I sank into your folds,
or salved your pastel tits,
but could not come.

Sexless as a pimp
dying in performance
like a flare gone down,
the tooth of your pier
hones near the wharf.
The ocean is breathing,
its cautious insomnia—
driven here and there—
with only itself to love.

American History

Those four black girls blown up
in that Alabama church
remind me of five hundred
middle passage blacks,
in a net, under water
in Charleston harbor
so *redcoats* wouldn't find them.
Can't find what you can't see
can you?

A Mother Speaks:
The Algiers Motel Incident, Detroit

It's too dark to see black
in the windows of Woodward
or Virginia Park.
The undertaker
pushed his body back
into place

with plastic and gum
but it wouldn't
hold water.
When I looked
for marks
or lineament
or fine stitching
I was led away
without seeing
this plastic
face they'd built
that was not my son's.
They tied the eye
torn out
by shotgun
into place
and his shattered
arm cut away
with his buttocks
that remained.
My son's gone
by white hands
though he said
to his last word—
"Oh I'm so sorry,
officer, I broke your gun."

YUSEF IMAN

Love Your Enemy

Brought here in slave ships and pitched overboard.
Love your enemy
Language taken away, culture taken away
Love your enemy
Work from sun up to sun down
Love your enemy
Last hired, first fired
Love your enemy
Rape your mother
Love your enemy
Lynch your father
Love your enemy
Bomb your churches
Love your enemy
Kill your children
Love your enemy
Forced to fight his Wars
Love your enemy
Pay the highest rent
Love your enemy
Sell you rotten food
Love your enemy
Forced to live in the slums
Love your enemy
Dilapidated schools
Love your enemy
Puts you in jail
Love your enemy
Bitten by dogs
Love your enemy
Water hose you down

Love your enemy
Love,
Love,
Love,
Love,
Love, for everybody else,
     but when will we love ourselves?

DON L. LEE (1942–   )

BACK AGAIN, HOME

(confessions of an ex-executive)

Pains of insecurity surround me;
    shined shoes,
    conservative suits,
    button down shirts with silk ties.
    bi-weekly payroll.

Ostracized, but not knowing why;
    executive haircut,
    clean shaved,
    "yes" instead of "yeah" and "no" instead of "naw",
    hours, nine to five. (after five he's alone)

"Doing an excellent job, keep it up;"
    promotion made—semi-monthly payroll,
    very quiet—never talks,
    budget balanced—saved the company money,
    quality work—production tops.
    He looks sick. (but there is a smile in his eyes)

He resigned, we wonder why;
    let his hair grow—a mustache too,
    out of a job—broke and hungry,
    friends are coming back—bring food,
    not quiet now—trying to speak,
    what did he say?

    "Back Again,

        BLACK AGAIN,

                Home."

RE-ACT FOR ACTION

(for brother H. Rap Brown)

re-act to animals:
> cage them in zoos.

re-act to inhumanism:
> make them human.

re-eact to nigger toms:
> with spiritual acts of love & for-
> giveness or with real acts of force.

re-act to yr/self:
> or are u too busy tryen to be cool
> like tony curtis & twiggy?

re-act to whi-te actors:
> understand their actions;
> faggot actions & actions against yr/
> dreams

re-act to yr/brothers & sisters:
> love.

re-act to whi-te actions:
> with real acts of blk /action.
> BAM BAM BAM

re-act to act against actors
who act out pig-actions against
your acts & actions that keep
you re-acting against their act & actions
stop.
act in a way that will cause them
to act the way you want them to act
in accordance with yr/acts & actions:
> human acts for human beings

re-act
NOW niggers
& you won't have to
act
false-actions
at
your/children's graves.

THE PRIMITIVE

taken from the
shores of Mother Africa.
the savages they thought
we were—
they being the real savages.
to save us. (from what?)
our happiness, our love, each other?
their bible for
our land. (introduction to economics)
christianized us.
raped our minds with:
T.V. & straight hair,
Reader's Digest & bleaching creams,
tarzan & jungle jim,
used cars & used homes,
reefers & napalm,
european history & promises.
Those alien concepts
of whi-teness,
the being of what
is not.
against our nature,
this weapon called
civilization—
they brought us here—
to drive us mad.
(like them)

The Self-Hatred of Don L. Lee

i,
at one time,
loved
my
color—
it

opened sMall
doors of
tokenism
&
acceptance.

(doors called, "the only one" & "our negro")

after painfully
struggling
thru Du Bois,
Rogers, Locke,
Wright & others,
my blindness
was vanquished
by pitchblack
paragraphs of
"us, we, me, i"
awareness.

i
began
to love
only a
part of
me—
my inner
self which
is all
black—
&
developed a
vehement
hatred of
my light
brown
outer.

communication in whi-te

dee dee dee dee dee wee weee eeeeee wee we
    deweeeeeeee ee ee ee nig
nig nig nig niggggggggggggggggg cleek cleek cleek
    cleeeeee cleekcleek
rip rip rip rip rip/rip/rip/rip/rip/ ripripripripripripripripri
    pi pi pi pi pip
bom bom bom bom bom/bom/bom/bombombombom
    bombbombbombbombbombbomb
deathtocleekdeathtocleekdeathtocleekdeathtocleek
    deathtocleekdeathtodeathto
alllllllllllllalllllllllllll allll llllllll deathtoalllllllll alllllllll
    alllllleeeeeee
te te te te te te te/te/te/te/te/te/ tetetetetetetetetetete
    tetetetetetete:
the paris peace talks, 1968.

But He Was Cool
or: he even stopped for green lights

super-cool
ultrablack
a tan/purple
had a beautiful shade.

he had a double-natural
that wd put the sisters to shame.
his dashikis were tailor made
& his beads were imported sea shells
    (from some blk/country i never heard of)
he was triple-hip.

his tikis were hand carved
out of ivory
& came express from the motherland.
he would greet u in swahili
& say good-by in yoruba.

woooooooooooo-jim he bes so cool & ill tel li gent

> cool-cool is so cool he was un-cooled by other niggers' cool
> cool-cool ultracool was bop-cool/ice box cool so cool cold cool
> his wine didn't have to be cooled, him was air conditioned cool
> cool-cool/real cool made me cool—now ain't that cool
> cool-cool so cool him nick-named refrigerator.

cool-cool so cool
he didn't know,
after detroit, newark, chicago &c.,
we had to hip

> cool-cool/   super-cool/   real cool

      that
to be black
is
to be°
very-hot.

a poem to complement other poems

change.
like if u were a match i wd light u into something beautiful. change.
change.
for the better into a realreal together thing. change, from a make believe
nothing on corn meal and water. change.
change. from the last drop to the first, maxwellhouse did. change.
change was a programmer for IBM, thought him was a brown computer. change.

colored is something written on southern outhouses.
   change.
greyhound did, i mean they got rest rooms on buses.
   change.
change.
change nigger.
saw a nigger hippy, him wanted to be different. changed.
saw a nigger liberal, him wanted to be different. changed.
saw a nigger conservative, him wanted to be different.
   changed.
niggers don't u know that niggers are different. change.
a doublechange. nigger wanted a double zero in front of
   his name; a license to kill,
niggers are licensed to be killed. change. a negro: some-
   thing pigs eat.
change. i say change into a realblack righteous aim. like
   i don't play
saxophone but that doesn't mean i don't dig 'trane.'
   change.
hear u coming but yr/steps are too loud. change. even a
   lamp post changes nigger.
change, stop being an instant yes machine. change.
niggers don't change they just grow. that's a change;
   bigger & better niggers.
change, into a necessary blackself.
change, like a gas meter gets higher.
change, like a blues song talking about a righteous to-
   morrow.
change, like a tax bill getting higher.
change, like a good sister getting better.
change, like knowing wood will burn. change.
know the realenemy.
change,
change nigger: standing on the corner, thought him was
                          cool. him still
                  standing there. it's winter time, him cool.
change,
know the realenemy.

change: him wanted to be a TV star. him is. ten o'clock
    news.
        wanted, wanted. nigger stole some lemon & lime
        popsicles,
    thought them were diamonds.
change nigger change.
know the realenemy.
change: is u is or is u aint. change. now now change. for
    the better change.
        read a change. live a change. read a blackpoem.
        change. be the realpeople.
        change. blackpoems
will change:

know the realenemy. change. know the realenemy. change
    yr/enemy change know the real
change know the realenemy change, change, know the
    realenemy, the realenemy, the real
realenemy change your the enemies/change your change
    your change your enemy change
your enemy. know the realenemy, the world's enemy.
    know them know them know them the
realenemy change your enemy change your change
    change change your enemy change change
change change your change change change.
your
mind nigger.

One Sided Shoot-out

*(for brothers fred hampton & mark clark, murdered
12/4/69 by chicago police at 4:30 AM while they slept)*

only a few will really understand:
it won't be yr/mommas or yr/brothers & sisters or even
    me,
we all think that we do   but we don't.
it's not *new*   and

under all the rhetoric the seriousness is still not serious.
the national rap deliberately continues, "wipe them nig-
    gers out."
(no talk do it, no talk do it, no talk do it, notalk notalk-
    notalk do it)

& we.
running circleround getting caught in our own cobwebs,
in the same old clothes, same old words, just new adjec-
    tives.
we will order new buttons & posters with: "remember
    fred" & "rite-on mark."
& yr/pictures will be beautiful & manly with the deep-
    look/ the accusing look
to remind us
to remind us that suicide is not black.

the questions will be asked & the answers will be the new
    cliches.
but maybe,
just maybe we'll finally realize that "revolution" to the
    real-world
is international 24hours a day and that 4:30AM is like
    12:00 noon,
it's just darker.
but the evil can be seen if u look in the right direction.
were the street lights out?
did they darken their faces in combat?
did they remove their shoes to *creep* softer?
could u not see the whi-te of their eyes,
the whi-te of their deathfaces?
didn't yr/look-out man see them coming, coming, coming?
or did they turn into ghostdust and join the night's fog?

it was mean.
& we continue to call them "pigs" and "muthafuckas"
    forgetting what all
black children learn very early: "sticks & stones may break
                                my bones but names can
                                never hurt me."

it was murder.
& we meet to hear the speeches/ the same, the duplica-
    tors.
they say that which is expected of them.
to be instructive or constructive is to be unpopular (like:
    the leaders only
sleep when there is a watchingeye)
but they say the right things at the right time, it's like a
    stageshow:
only the entertainers have changed.
we remember bobby hutton. the same, the duplicators.

the seeing eye should always see.
the night doesn't stop the stars
& our enemies scope the ways of blackness in three bad
    shifts a day.
in the AM their music becomes deadlier.
this is a game of dirt.

only blackpeople play it fair.

Big Momma

finally retired   pensionless
from cleaning somebody else's house
she remained home to clean
the one she didn't own.

in her kitchen where we often talked
the *chicago tribune* served as a tablecloth
for the two cups of tomato soup that went
along with my weekly visit & talkingto.

she was in a seriously-funny mood
& from the get-go she was down, realdown:

        roaches around here are like
        letters on a newspaper

or
u gonta be a writer, hunh
when u gone write me some writen
or
the way niggers act around here
if talk cd kill we'd all be dead.

she's somewhat confused about all this *blackness*
but said that it's good when negroes start putting them-
selves
first and added: we've always shopped at the colored
stores,
& the way niggers cut each other up
round here every weekend that white-
man don't haveta
worry bout no revolution specially
when he's gonna haveta pay for it too,
anyhow all he's gotta do is drop a
truck load of *dope* out there
on 43rd st. & all the niggers & yr
revolutionaries
be too busy getten high & then they'll
turn round
and fight each other over who got the
mostest.

we finished our soup and i moved to excuse myself,
as we walked to the front door she made a last com-
ment:
now *luther* i knows you done changed a lots but if
you can think back, we never did eat too much pork
round here anyways, it was bad for the belly.
i shared her smile and agreed.

touching the snow lightly i headed for 43rd st.
at the corner i saw a brother crying   while
trying to hold up a lamp post,
thru his watery eyes i cd see big momma's words.

at sixty-eight
she moves freely, is often right
and when there is food
eats   joyously with her own
real teeth.

Mixed Sketches

u feel that way sometimes
wondering:
as a nine year old sister
with burned out hair oddly
smiles at you and sweetly calls you
brother

u feel that way sometimes
wondering:
as a blackwoman & her 6 children
are burned out of their apartment with no place
to go & a nappy-headed nigger comes running thru
our neighborhood with a match in his hand cryin
revolution

u feel that way sometimes
wondering:
seeing sisters in two hundred dollar wigs & suits
fastmoving in black clubs in late surroundings   talking
about late thoughts in late language waiting for late men
that come in with, "i don't want to hear bout nothing
    black tonight."

u feel that way sometimes
wondering:
while eating on newspaper tablecloths
& sleeping on clean bed sheets that couldn't
stop bed bugs   as black children watch their
mothers leave the special buses returning from

special neighborhoods
to clean their "own" unspecial homes.

u feel that way sometimes
wondering:
wondering, how did we survive?

We Walk the Way of the New World

1.

we run the dangercourse.
the way of the stocking caps & murray's grease.
(if u is modern u used duke greaseless hair pomade)
jo jo was modern/ an international nigger
                    born: jan. 1, 1863 in new york, mississippi.
his momma was mo militant than he was/ is
jo jo bes no instant negro
his development took all of 106 years
& he was the first to be stamped "made in USA"
where he arrived bow-legged a curve ahead of the 20th
    century's new weapon: television.
which invented, "how to win and influence people"
& gave jo jo his how/ ever look: however u want me.

we discovered that with the right brand of cigarettes
that one, with his best girl,
cd skip thru grassy fields in living color
& in slow-motion: Caution: niggers, cigarette smoking
                    will kill u & yr/health.
& that the breakfast of champions is: blackeyed peas &
    rice.
& that God is dead & Jesus is black and last seen on 63rd
            street in a gold & black dashiki, sitting in a
            pink hog speaking swahili with a pig-latin
            accent.
& that integration and coalition are synonymous,

& that the only thing that really mattered was:
   who could get the highest on the least or how to ex-
   pand & break one's mind.

in the coming world
new prizes are
to be given

we *ran* the dangercourse,
now, it's a silent walk/ a careful eye
jo jo is there
to his mother he is unknown
(she accepted with a newlook: what wd u do if someone
   loved u?)
jo jo is back
& he will catch all the new jo jo's as they wander in & out
and with a fan-like whisper say: you ain't no
                          tourist
                          and Harlem ain't for
                          sight-seeing, brother.

                       2.

Start with the itch and there will be no scratch. Study
   yourself.
Watch yr/every movement as u skip thru-out the south-
   side of chicago.
be hip to yr/actions.

our dreams are realities
traveling the nature-way.
we meet them
at the apex of their utmost
meanings/means;
we walk in cleanliness
down state st/or Fifth Ave.
& wicked apartment buildings shake
as their windows announce our presence
as we jump into the interior
& cut the day's evil away.

We walk in cleanliness
the newness of it all
becomes us
our women listen to us
and learn.
We teach our children thru
our actions.

We'll become owners of the   New World
the New World.
will run it as unowners
for
we will live in it too
& will want to be remembered
as   realpeople.

DOUGHTRY LONG (1942–)

Ginger Bread Mama

i love you ginger bread mama
ginger bread mama
                        all sweet and brown
love you
            more than tired boys
love collard greens and candied yams
more than new watermelons
                                    do the sun.

before you,
i was older
                and owned a sky of sleep
and not even cowboy dreams
were poets enough to wish me you.
now in brownness warm
everything is everything and
our forms move in soft affirmations.
trying not to wake up the sun.

One Time Henry
Dreamed the Number

one time henry dreamed the number
but we didn't play it,
and do you know, that thing came out straight
3-67?
        yes it did!
we was both sick
for a whole week,
                could'a sure used
                            the money then too.

that was back in hoover's time
when folks was scufflin
to make ends meet.
i knock on wood though
                    we've lived through it all.
last night after we ate
the last of the meat loaf and greens
and was watching television
henry asked me if i rememberded that,
i told him yes,
            we laughed
                    then went to bed
and kept each other warm.

EVERETT HOAGLAND (1942–   )

love Child—a black aesthetic

sweet baked apple dappled cinnamon speckled sin of
   mine
nutmeg freckled peach brandy and amber wine woman
   WOW
with your piping hot and finger popping black african
pepper pot not stopping steaming coffee flowing cream-
   ing
the brown sugar growing cane candy coming cocoa going
crazy 'bout brown sugar teases GOOD GOD and pleases
   SWEET
JESUS that honey stained soul trained slow molasses ass
and GODDAMN candied yam and sweet potatoe pie
thighs and sweet raisin tipped coconut tits raising cane
   sugar
stone brown sugar bowl belly to the bone to the bone

in in rhythm with life rhythms without metronomes
   dance
too well together in the horizontal harvest dance dance
of the slurp slap sea bellies rapid clapping rhapsody in
the seeds' ceremony through the tangled jungle vines we
love in comely comes this black cat night purring in ears
of our now we love earth humming bird humming under
the back and black of our now we love tuning fork
   thighs taut
vibrant bread loaves alive for me on the crest of our now
we love screaming and curdled creaming cradled in
   crisis
of our now we love now we love now my love now my
   love now my love
love me now my love my love My Love NOW! !

glob globs of tapioca textured essence of nascence ice-
cream
fire yellow white hot maggots seeming more than semen
sperm jellied germ of god the rich pudding of love tiring
tadpole
couriers of destiny coursing toward the heaven halo
aborrea
of egg sun like yolk wonder deep in the night time of
belly love

the moontide stops womb waves of life wine time savors
remembered good love and gourd opulent dark pump-
kin belly
harvest of love swollen organic sacristy abode to ex-
quisite
profanity

POP! ! a black pearl from god brand new small brown
sugar
lump velvet little wild rabbit burnished gold nugget rock
a
bye rock a bye sweet blackberry pie and honey love
syrup
soul soft fur brown round little cup of rum nectarous
distillation of the words "i love you" . . . godly milky
mystical
nascency succulent miracle

My Spring Thing

yes, yes
it's time
to do my spring thing
hanging
around the sweet and the green
flowing
up warm sap
rising
days of

being fresh as April and
common as grass

yes, yes
it's spring
to do my time slow
as the bulbs burst
from the scrotal earth
while
the gay and golden sun sighs
over the bright dick daffodils'
stiff erections

yes, yes
it's my thing to time
my spring
by the frequency of small
patches of black
grass in the splendor
of thighs
without words—
worth

The Anti-Semanticist

honeystain . . .
the rhetoricians of blackness
matters me not
we are black
and you are beautiful

it matters me not whether
your breasts are american pumpkin or
african gourds
they are full and you are beautiful

it matters me not be your belly
black or brown
it is soft and you are beautiful

it matters me not be your buttocks
bourgeois or "grass roots"
they are good
and you are beautiful

it matters me not if your bread loaf
thighs
are negro or afro-american
they are round and so ripe
and you are so beautiful

it matters not whether it is
Victoria falls within your orgasms
instead of Niagara

there is little definition i need
indeed
it matters only that there is
black power
in your loving

this i know

you are beautiful
you are beautiful beyond reference
you are the night interpreted
you are
you

It's a Terrible Thing!

opulent oracle—it's a terrible thing!
my, my
pink and purple butterfly
fine as you want to be!

sly sleepin' creamy creepin' soul stabbin' dippin'
dabbin' slick dick grabbin' slack cuttin'

suede buttoned do it to it bringin' fluid
soft socking "Deep River" rocking big leg cocking cock
                                        it's a terrible thing!

like a laser beamin'
hot coffee steamin'
nut butter creamin'
it's the only dream that COMES
(true i.e.),
            it's a terrible thing!

Conceived in Eden, sustained in Africa, hybrid
in America
            it's a terrible thing!

move to: south side
            Cottage Grove groove
            on Euclid Ave, its Erie and hypnotic
            strokes make Black votes for Stokes
            Philly's 52nd St. ("strip") party-dip
            can get you higher than the
            market st. "El"
            hell! in Harlem sweet
            sugar-hill holes are brown
            sugar bowls used for cooking
            it's too mean in Boston!
            molasses bean casser-hole
            and there ain't no more in Baltimore
            than they know what to do with
            over in A.C. its sunbaked sandcaked
            water-wet bikini revelation can get you
            harder than a chicken bone
            beach
            peaches in Atlanta don't grow
            on trees
            and their pits are full of the devil
            it gets down northeast nasty
            in D.C.—it's a terrible thing!

yeah!   it's a beast back east
    but it's at its golden bay
    best in the west
    (L.A. stands for—lord! Allelujia! !)
                it's a terrible thing!

    glistenin' a doughnut glazed and gluey
    it could even free Huey
    it's a dewy black rose
    it's a terrible thing!

    like the lord
    it's laid in a manger

    mounted in the saddle
    of sigh-making thighs
    framed by sky blues
    rhythm hips heaving rock and roll—
    GET IT! !—backed by Black
    buttocks the best to the bone
                it's a terrible thing!

    less catacomb
    than honey-comb
    more pleasure dome than Kubla Khan
    cock is more pleasing than pleasure is
    is box, is cunt, is piece o'ass, is twat, is slit,
    is slat, is snatch, is fuzzburger, is jelly-roll
    is PUSSY, is a motherfucker! !
                it's a terrible thing!

    and just like the folks told King Jesus
    it's telling more than a tail
    it makes a Brother
    "ride on! !"—RIGHT ON! ! !
    (it's a terrible thing!)

NIKKI GIOVANNI (1943–   )

The True Import of Present Dialogue: Black vs. Negro

(For Peppi, Who Will Ultimately Judge Our Efforts)

Nigger
Can you kill
Can you kill
Can a nigger kill
Can a nigger kill a honkie
Can a nigger kill the Man
Can you kill nigger
Huh? nigger can you
kill
Do you know how to draw blood
Can you poison
Can you stab-a-jew
Can you kill huh? nigger
Can you kill
Can you run a protestant down with your
'68 El Dorado
(that's all they're good for anyway)
Can you kill
Can you piss on a blond head
Can you cut it off
Can you kill
A nigger can die
We ain't got to prove we can die
We got to prove we can kill
They sent us to kill
Japan and Africa
We policed europe
Can you kill
Can you kill a white man

Can you kill the nigger
in you
Can you make your nigger mind
die
Can you kill your nigger mind
And free your black hands to
strangle
Can you kill
Can a nigger kill
Can you shoot straight and
Fire for good measure
Can you splatter their brains in the street
Can you kill them
Can you lure them to bed to kill them
We kill in Viet Nam
for them
We kill for UN & NATO & SEATO & US
And everywhere for all alphabet but
BLACK
Can we learn to kill WHITE for BLACK
Learn to kill niggers
Learn to be Black men

1–'68

My Poem

i am 25 years old
black female poet
wrote a poem asking
nigger can you kill
if they kill me
it won't stop
the revolution

i have been robbed
it looked like they knew
that i was to be hit

they took my tv
my two rings
my piece of african print
and my two guns
if they take my life
it won't stop   if i never write
the revolution   another poem
                                                 or short story
my phone is tapped   if i flunk out
my mail is opened   of grad school
they've caused me to turn   if my car is reclaimed
on all my old friends   and my record player
and all my new lovers   won't play
if i hate all black   and if i never see
people   a peaceful day
and all negroes   or do a meaningful
it won't stop   black thing
the revolution   it won't stop
                                                 the revolution

i'm afraid to tell
my roommate where i'm going   the revolution
and scared to tell   is in the streets
people if i'm coming   and if i stay on
if i sit here   the 5th floor
for the rest   it will go on
of my life   if i never do
if won't stop   anything
the revolution   it will go on

                                        10–3–'68

Beautiful Black Men (*with compliments and apologies
to all not mentioned by name*)

i wanta say just gotta say something
bout those beautiful beautiful beautiful outasight
black men
with they afros
walking down the street

is the same ol danger
but a brand new pleasure

sitting on stoops, in bars, going to offices
running numbers, watching for their whores
preaching in churches, driving their hogs
walking their dogs, winking at me
in their fire red, lime green, burnt orange
royal blue tight tight pants that hug
what i like to hug

jerry butler, wilson pickett, the impressions
temptations, mighty mighty sly
don't have to do anything but walk
on stage
and i scream and stamp and shout
see new breed men in breed alls
dashiki suits with shirts that match
the lining that compliments the ties
that smile at the sandals
where dirty toes peek at me
and i scream and stamp and shout
for more beautiful beautiful beautiful
black men with outasight afros

9–10–'68

For Saundra

i wanted to write
a poem
that rhymes
but revolution doesn't lend
itself to be-bopping

then my neighbor
who thinks i hate
asked—do you ever write

tree poems—i like trees
so i thought
i'll write a beautiful green tree poem
peeked from my window
to check the image
noticed the school yard was covered
with asphalt
no green—no trees grow
in manhattan

then, well, i thought the sky
i'll do a big blue sky poem
but all the clouds have winged
low since no-Dick was elected

so i thought again
and it occurred to me
maybe i shouldn't write
at all
but clean my gun
and check my kerosene supply

perhaps these are not poetic
times
at all

Knoxville, Tennessee

I always like summer
best
you can eat fresh corn
from daddy's garden
and okra
and greens
and cabbage
and lots of
barbecue
and buttermilk
and homemade ice-cream

at the church picnic
and listen to
gospel music
outside
at the church
homecoming
and go to the mountains with
your grandmother
and go barefooted
and be warm
all the time
not only when you go to bed
and sleep

5–17–'68

The Funeral of Martin Luther King, Jr.

His headstone said
FREE AT LAST, FREE AT LAST
But death is a slave's freedom
We seek the freedom of free men
And the construction of a world
Where Martin Luther King could have lived and
    preached non-violence

Atlanta
4–9–'68

Concerning One Responsible Negro
with Too Much Power

scared?
are responsible negros running
scared?

i understand I'm to be sued
and you say you can't fight fifteen hundred national
    guards

men
so you'll beat the shit
out of poor Black me
(no doubt because I've castrated you)

dynamite came to your attention
and responsible negros tell the cops

your tongue must be removed
since you have no brain
to keep it in check

aren't you turned around
teaching tolerance
how can I tolerate
genocide
my cup is full
and you already know
we have no ability
to delay gratification

i only want to reclaim myself
i even want you
to reclaim yourself
but more and more i'm being convinced
that your death
responsible negro
is the first step
toward my reclamation

its very sad
i'd normally stop and cry
but evening is coming
and i've got to negotiate
for my people's freedom

4–3–'68

Poem for Black Boys

(With Special Love To James)

Where are your heroes, my little Black ones
You are the indian you so disdainfully shoot
Not the big bad sheriff on his faggoty white horse

You should play run-away-slave
or Mau Mau
These are more in line with your history

Ask your mothers for a Rap Brown gun
Santa just may comply if you wish hard enough
Ask for CULLURD instead of Monopoly
DO NOT SIT IN DO NOT FOLLOW KING
GO DIRECTLY TO STREETS
This is a game you can win

As you sit there with your all understanding eyes
You know the truth of what I'm saying
Play Back-to-Black
Grow a natural and practice vandalism
These are useful games (some say a skill is even learned)

There is a new game I must tell you of
Its called Catch The Leader Lying
(and knowing your sense of the absurd you will enjoy
this)

Also a company called Revolution has just issued a
special kit for little boys called Burn Baby
I'm told it has full instructions on how to siphon gas
and fill a bottle

Then our old friend Hide and Seek becomes valid
Because we have much to seek and ourselves to hide
from a lecherous dog

And this poem I give is worth much more than any
nickle bag
or ten cent toy
And you will understand all too soon
That you, my children of battle, are your heroes
You must invent your own games and teach us old ones
how to play

4–2–'67

Kidnap Poem

ever been kidnapped
by a poet
if i were a poet
i'd kidnap you

put you in my phrases
and meter you to jones beach
or maybe coney island
or maybe just to my house

lyric you in lilacs
dash you in the rain
alliterate the beach
to complement my see

play the lyre for you
ode you with my love song
anything to win you
wrap you in the red Black green
show you off to mama

yeah if i were
a poet i'd kid
nap you

Poem for Aretha

cause nobody deals with aretha—a mother with four chil-
    dren—
having to hit the road
they always say "after she comes
home" but nobody ever says what it's like
to get on a plane for a three week tour
the elation of the first couple of audiences the good
feeling of exchange the running on the high
you get from singing good
and loud and long telling the world
what's on your mind

then comes the eighth show on the sixth day the begin-
    ning
to smell like the plane or bus the if-you-forget-your-
    toothbrush
in-one-spot-you-can't-brush-until-the-second-show   the
    strangers
pulling at you cause they love you but you having no love
to give back
the singing the same songs night after night day after day
and if you read the gossip columns the rumors that your
    husband
is only after your fame
the wondering if your children will be glad to see you
    and maybe
the not caring if they are the scheming to get
out of just one show and go just one place where some
    doe-doe-dupaduke
won't say "just sing one song, please"

nobody mentions how it feels to become a freak
because you have talent and how
no one gives a damn how you feel
but only cares that aretha franklin is here like maybe
    that'll stop
        chickens from frying
        eggs from being laid
        crackers from hating

and if you say you're lonely or tired how they always
just say "oh come off it" or "did you see
how they loved you did you see huh did you?"
which most likely has nothing to do with you anyway
and i'm not saying aretha shouldn't have talent and i'm
  certainly
not saying she should quit
singing but as much as i love her i'd vote "yes" to her
doing four concerts a year and staying home or doing
  whatever
she wants and making records cause it's a shame
the way we're killing her
we eat up artists like there's going to be a famine at the
  end
of those three minutes when there are in fact an abun-
  dance
of talents just waiting let's put some
of the giants away for a while and deal with them like
  they have
a life to lead

aretha doesn't have to relive billie holiday's life doesn't
  have
to relive dinah washington's death but who will
stop the pattern

she's more important than her music—if they must be
  separated—
and they should be separated when she has to pass out
  before
anyone recognizes she needs
a rest and i say i need
aretha's music
she is undoubtedly the one person who put everyone on
notice
she revived johnny ace and remembered lil green aretha
  sings
"i say a little prayer" and dionne doesn't
want to hear it anymore
aretha sings "money won't change you"

but james can't sing "respect" the advent
of aretha pulled ray charles from marlboro country
and back into
the blues made nancy wilson
try one more time forced
dionne to make a choice (she opted for the movies)
and diana ross had to get an afro wig pushed every
Black singer into his Blackness and negro entertainers
into negroness you couldn't jive
when she said "you make me/feel" the blazers
had to reply "gotta let a man be/a man"
aretha said "when my show was in the lost and found/
    you came
along to claim it" and joplin said "maybe"
there has been no musician whom her very presence
    hasn't
affected when humphrey wanted her to campaign for
    him she said
"woman's only human"
and he pressured james brown
they removed otis cause the combination was too strong
the impressions had to say "lord have mercy/we're mov-
    ing
on up"
the Black songs started coming from the singers on stage
    and the dancers
in the streets
aretha was the riot was the leader if she had said "come
let's do it" it would have been done
temptations say why don't we think about it
                        think about it
                        think about it

STEPHANY (1947–   )

In the Silence

In the silence
of the city night
when the lonely
watch the sky
in yearning

I at rest
beside you
lie in peace

I searched
a thousand skies
before you came

And in the morning
when the world
is new,
the lonely turn
away

as I turn to
you beside
me

And in the quiet
of the afternoon
when the lonely
roam,

I turn inside
and you
are with me still

I roamed
a thousand miles
before you came.

Who Is Not a Stranger Still

Who is not a stranger still
even after making love,
or the morning after?

The interlude of sleep again divides
it is clear again where one body
ends and the next begins,

Think to think at each encounter,
we will be strangers still
even after making love
and long conversation,
even after meals and showers
together

and years of touching.
It is not often that the core
of what I am is lost in longing

and is less often filled.
I understand my clinging
to the thought of you.

My Love When This Is Past

My love when this is past
and you have turned away
—or I

and we are no longer
as we are today
I will be more

having known your love
I will be more
and not alone.

Let Me Be Held When the Longing Comes

Let me be held when the longing comes
by you

Yours the arms, yours the tender
breath.

Tumble down into the quiet dark
of this embrace
night is come again.

Stay a little longer,
for no other reason than it is
good not to be alone always
let there be a song of
remembering and not knowing
what is there except
a warmth and a blossom
of a feeling, sweetly,
gladly, home.

That We Head Towards

That we head towards
our separate End
and know it only
by the name of Death . . .

But makes this life
with you more dear.
And having known
this joy and you
so tender

without a fear
I face this life
so beautiful

and in the End
will with pain
surrender

the sight,
the touch,
or memory
of You.

PUBLISHERS OF BLACK POETRY

Afro-Arts, Inc. Publisher: Don Holder. 37 W. 20th St., New York, N.Y. 10011.

Associated Publishers. Association for the Study of Negro Life and History. 1538 Ninth St., N.W., Washington, D.C. 20001. Published Robert Thomas Kerlin's important *Negro Poets and Their Poems,* children's poetry.

Blkartsouth. Editor: Tom Dent. 1716 N. Miro St., New Orleans, La. 70119. Published the literary magazine *Nkombo* and books of poetry for the Free Southern Theatre. *Nkombo* is now independent.

Black Academy Review Press, Inc. Editor: S. Okechukwu Mezu. Box 366, Ellicott Station, Buffalo, N.Y. 14205. Publishes the *Black Academy Review,* books.

Black Arts Publications. Editor: Ahmed Akinwole Alhamisi. 3484 Ewald Circle, Detroit, Mich. 48204. Publishes books and the anthology *Black Arts,* which is distributed by Broadside Press.

Black Dialogue Press. Editors: Ed Spriggs and Nikki Giovanni. Box 953, Manhattan Station, New York, N.Y. 10027. Published the literary magazine *Black Dialogue,* with Joe Goncalves as the able poetry editor, books. Now quiescent.

Black Liberation Publishers. East Palo Alto, Calif.

Black Star Publishers. 8824 Fenkell St., Detroit, Mich. 48238.

Paul Breman, Ltd. 7 Wedderburn Rd., London, N.W.3, England. Paul Breman's Heritage Series was the first (1962) to publish black poets on a continuing basis. He has published the anthology *Sixes and Sevens* and books by Robert Hayden, Ishmael Reed, Arna Bontemps, Frank Horne, Dudley Randall, Owen Dodson, Ray Durem, James Thompson, and others. Distributed in the United States by Broadside Press.

Broadside Press. Editor: Dudley Randall. 12651 Old Mill Pl., Detroit, Mich. 48238. Broadsides, books, tapes, records, posters. Besides poetry, publishes children's books and the Broadside Critics Series. Has published books by Gwendolyn

Brooks, Margaret Walker, Don L. Lee, Sonia Sanchez, Nikki Giovanni, Etheridge Knight, and many other leading poets.

Circle Press. Editor: Robert Bowen, 3026 Wellington Rd., Los Angeles, Calif. 90016.

Drum and Spear Press. Editor: Carolyn Carter. 1902 Belmont Rd., N.W., Washington, D.C. 20009. Also based in East Africa. Plans a bibliographical magazine. Has published an anthology of Palestinian poetry and children's books.

DuSable Museum of Afro-American History. Publisher: Margaret Burroughs. 3806 S. Michigan Ave., Chicago, Ill. 60653. Books, broadsides, phonograph records, prints, calendars, often illustrated by Margaret Burroughs, who is a painter and graphic artist.

Emerson Hall Publishers, Inc. Editor: Alfred E. Prettyman. 209 W. 97th St., New York, N.Y. 10025.

Free Black Press. Editor: Eugene Perkins. 7850 S. Cottage Grove Ave., Chicago, Ill. 60619. Books, *Black Expression*, a quarterly literary magazine (2 issues).

Free Lance Press. Editors: Casper Jordan and Russell Atkins. 5000 Grand Ave., Cleveland, Ohio 44104. Publishes the semi-yearly *Free Lance*, the oldest (1950) black poetry magazine. Books.

Free Southern Theatre (See Blkartsouth)

Jihad Productions. Publisher: Imamu Amiri Baraka. P.O. Box 663, Newark, New Jersey 07103. Books, broadsides, posters, records. Published LeRoi Jones, Clarence Reed, Yusef Iman.

Johnson Publishing Company. Editor: John H. Johnson. 1820 S. Michigan Ave., Chicago, Ill. 60616. The giant of Negro publishing. Publishes books and the magazines *Ebony, Jet, Tan,* and *Black World* (formerly *Negro Digest*). Has Ebony Book Club. In February 1971, published its first book of poetry, the anthology honoring Gwendolyn Brooks, *To Gwen with Love*.

Journal of Black Poetry Press. Editor: Joe Goncalves. 922 Haight St., Apt. B, San Francisco, Calif. 94117. Publishes the quarterly *Journal of Black Poetry*, the foremost black poetry magazine. Books.

Oduduwa Productions, Inc. University of Pittsburgh, Black Studies Department, Pittsburgh, Pa. 15213.

Julian Richardson Associates. Oakland, Calif.

Shabazz Publishing Company, 540 McAllister St., San Francisco, Calif. 94102.

The Third Press. Editor: Joseph Okpaku. 444 Central Park West, New York, N.Y. 10025.

Third World Press. Editor: Don L. Lee. 7850 S. Ellis Ave., Chicago, Ill. 60619. Publishes broadsides and books. Plans a bibliographical magazine, *Black Books Bulletin*. Has published Carolyn Rodgers, Ebon, Johari Amini, Sterling Plumpp, Dudley Randall, Amiri Baraka, and Sam Greenlee.

Vibration Press. Editor: Norman Jordan. P.O. Box 08152, Cleveland, Ohio 44108.

PERIODICALS PUBLISHING BLACK POETRY

AFRICA TODAY. Editors: George W. Sheperd and Ezekiel Mphahlele. Africa Today Associates, c/o Graduate School of International Studies, University of Denver, Denver, Colo. 80210. Bimonthly. $6.50 yearly, $1.50 single issue. Book reviews, advertisements, index. Indexed in PAIS.

BLACK AMERICA. Editor and publisher: J. Morris Anderson. Fashionable Publications, Inc., 245 W. Chelten Ave., Philadelphia, Pa. 19144.

BLACK ARTS MAGAZINE. Publisher: David Rambeau. 401 E. Adams, Detroit, Mich. 48226. Semiannual. $3.00 yearly, $1.50 single issue. Illustrations, book and play reviews, essays on black art. Has had guest editors. Students' work invited.

THE BLACK COLLEGIAN. Editor: N. R. Davidson. 3212 Melpomene St., New Orleans, La. 70125.

BLACK CREATION. Editor: Fred Beauford. Institute of Afro-American Affairs, New York University, Washington Square, N.Y. 10003. Quarterly. $4.00 yearly, $1.00 single issue. Photographs, drama reviews.

BLACK DIALOGUE. Editors: Abdul Karim and Ed Spriggs. P.O. Box 1019, New York, N.Y. 10027. Quarterly. $3.50 yearly, $1.00 single issue. Has published much fine poetry, probably because percipient Joe Goncalves is poetry editor, and the other editors are also poets.

BLACK ORPHEUS: A JOURNAL OF AFRICAN AND AFRO-AMERICAN LITERATURE. Editor: John Pepper Clark. Longman's of Nigeria, P.M.B. 1036, Ikeja, Nigeria. Irregular publication. $1.50 single issue. Book reviews.

BLACK PANTHER. P.O. Box 841, Emeryville Branch, Oakland, Calif. 94608. Biweekly. $5.50 yearly, $.25 single issue.

THE BLACK SCHOLAR: JOURNAL OF BLACK STUDIES AND RESEARCH. Editor: Robert Chrisman. Box 31245, Sausalito, Calif. 94965. Monthly except July and August. $6.00 yearly to students, $10.00 to nonstudents, $1.25 single issue.

BLACK THEATRE: A PERIODICAL OF THE BLACK THEATRE MOVEMENT. Editor: Ed Bullins. Room 103, 200 W. 135th St.,

New York, N.Y. 10030. Six times yearly. $1.50 yearly, $.35 single issue.

BLACK WORLD (formerly NEGRO DIGEST). Editor: Hoyt W. Fuller. 1820 S. Michigan Ave., Chicago, Ill. 60616. Monthly. $5.00 yearly, $.50 single issue. Index. Indexed in *Index to Negro Periodicals*. Book and record reviews. The foremost black literary magazine. Editor has a wide taste and does not restrict magazine to cliques or regions. September issue is annual poetry number. Magazine gives literary prizes. Pays for poetry.

BROADSIDE SERIES. Editor: Dudley Randall. 12651 Old Mill Pl., Detroit, Mich. 48238. Monthly. $6.00 yearly, $.50 single issue. Broadsheets containing one or more poems. Publishes the best black poetry of both new and established writers. Pays for poetry.

COLD TRUTH. Editor: Kattie M. Cumbo. 156 Fifth Ave., Suite 1229, New York, N.Y. 10010. Monthly. $6.00 yearly, $.75 monthly. Unsolicited material is encouraged, from both experienced and beginning writers. Token payments.

CONFRONTATION: A JOURNAL OF THIRD WORLD LITERATURE. Editor: Quincy Troupe. Black Studies Institute, Ohio University, Athens, Ohio 45701. Three times yearly. $5.00 yearly, $2.00 single issue. Photographs, book reviews.

CRICKET: BLACK MUSIC IN EVOLUTION. Editors: Imamu Amiri Baraka, Larry Neal, and A. B. Spellman. Box 663, Newark, N.J. Bimonthly. $5.00 yearly, $1.75 single issue.

THE CRISIS. Editor: Henry Lee Moon. 1790 Broadway, New York, N.Y. 10019. 10 times yearly. $3.50 yearly, $.25 single issue. Book reviews. Index. Indexed in *Index to Negro Periodicals, Readers' Guide to Periodical Literature*. THE CRISIS, with OPPORTUNITY, was one of the chief outlets for poets during the Harlem Renaissance. Publishes poetry only occasionally now.

DASEIN: THE QUARTERLY REVIEW. Editor: Percy Johnston. G.P.O. Box 2121, New York, N.Y. 10001. $3.50 yearly, $1.00 quarterly. Book, film, and play reviews. Index.

ESSENCE. Editor: Marcia Gillespie. 102 E. 30th St., New York, N.Y. 10016. Monthly. $6.00 yearly, $.60 single issue. A new magazine. Has published leading black poets. Pays generously for poetry.

FREE LANCE: A MAGAZINE OF POETRY AND PROSE. Editors: Casper LeRoy Jordan and Russell Atkins. 6005 Grand Ave., Cleveland, Ohio 44104. Twice yearly. $2.00 yearly, $1.00 single issue. Book reviews. The oldest black poetry magazine, founded in 1950.

FREEDOMWAYS. Editor: Esther Johnson. 799 Broadway, Suite 544. New York, N.Y. 10003. Quarterly. $3.50 yearly, $1.25 single issue. Book reviews. Index. Indexed in *Index to Negro Periodicals*.

JOURNAL OF BLACK POETRY. Editor: Joe Goncalves. 922 Haight St., Apt. B, San Francisco, Calif. 94117. Quarterly. $4.00 yearly, $1.25 single issue. Book reviews, interviews, news of poets and poetry. The leading black poetry magazine. Has had special African and children's issues. Guest editors have been Don Lee. Sonia Sanchez, Clarence Major, Ed Spriggs, Larry Neal, Dudley Randall, and Askia Muhammed Touré.

LIBERATOR. Editor: Daniel H. Watts. 244 E. 46th St., New York, N.Y. 10017. Monthly. $3.00 yearly. $.35 single issue. Book and drama reviews, photographs. Pays for poetry.

NEGRO DIGEST (see BLACK WORLD)

THE NEGRO HISTORY BULLETIN. Editor: Charles H. Wesley. 1538 Ninth St., N.W., Washington, D.C. 20001. Published eight times yearly. $3.50 yearly, $1.00 single issue. Book reviews. Indexed in *Readers' Guide to Periodical Literature* and *Index to Negro Periodicals*.

NKOMBO. Editors: Kush (Tom Dent) and Kalamu Ya Salaam (Val Ferdinand). Nkombo Publications, P.O. Box 51826, New Orleans, La. 70150. Quarterly. $4.00 yearly, $1.00 single issue.

NOMMO: THE JOURNAL OF THE OBAC WRITERS' WORKSHOP. Editor: Hoyt W. Fuller. 77 E. 35th St., Chicago, Ill. 60616. Quarterly. $4.00 yearly, $1.00 single issue. Publishes poets of the OBAC (Organization of Black American Culture) Writers' Workshop. Does not solicit poetry from nonmembers.

OKYEAME: GHANA'S LITERARY MAGAZINE. Editor: Efua Sutherland. Half-yearly. $1.50 yearly, $.75 single issue. Includes translations into English of African poetry (Ewe and other languages).

OUR VOICE. Editor: Tommy Wright. 901 College St., N.W., Knoxville, Tenn. 37921. Monthly. $6.00 yearly, $.50 single issue. Book reviews.

PATTERNS: NEWSLETTER OF THE INSTITUTE FOR BLACK STUDIES. Editor: Lucille Bowen. 3026 Wellington Rd., Los Angeles, Calif. 90016. Bimonthly. $3.50 yearly, $.75 single issue.

PHYLON. Editor: Tilman C. Cothran. 223 Chestnut St., S.W., Atlanta, Ga. 30314. Quarterly. $4.50 yearly, $1.50 single issue. Book reviews. Index. Indexed in *Index to Negro Periodicals, Readers' Guide to Periodical Literature*.

PRÉSENCE AFRICAINE; REVUE CULTURELLE DU MONDE NOIRE. Editor: Alioune Diop. 25 bis rue des Écoles, Paris (5e), France. Quarterly. $5.50 yearly, $1.00 single issue. French and English editions. Book reviews.

RHYTHM. Editor: Donald Stone. 859½ Hunter St., N.W., Atlanta, Ga. 30314. Quarterly. $4.00 yearly, $1.25 single issue.

SOULBOOK. Editor: Mamadou Lumumba. P.O. Box 1097, Berkeley, Calif. 94701. Quarterly. $3.00 yearly, $1.00 single issue. Book reviews.

TAN. Editor: Ariel P. Strong. 1820 S. Michigan Ave., Chicago, Ill. 60616. Monthly. $5.00 yearly, $.50 single issue. A confession magazine, it publishes love poetry.

THEATRE OF AFRO ARTS. Editors: W. Narcisse. P.O. Box 94, Northwest Branch, Miami, Fla. 33147.

UMBRA. Editor: David Henderson. P.O. Box 374, Peter Stuyvesant Station, New York, N.Y. 10009. Three times yearly. $3.00 yearly, $1.00 single issue.

VIBRATION. Editors: Norma Jean and Don Freeman. P.O. Box 08152, Cleveland, Ohio 44108.

PHONOGRAPH RECORDS

Collections

Anthology of Negro Poets. Folkways Records FL9791 2s 12". Edited by Arna Bontemps. Langston Hughes, Sterling Brown, Claude McKay, Countee Cullen, Margaret Walker, and Gwendolyn Brooks reading their own poetry.

Anthology of Negro Poets in the U.S.A.: 200 Years. Folkways Records FL9792 2s 12". Read by Arna Bontemps.

Been in the Storm so Long: Spirituals and Shouts, Children's Game Songs. Folkways Records FS3842.

Beyond the Blues: American Negro Poetry. Argo RG338 2s 12". Edited by Dr. Rosey E. Pool. Read by Vinette Carroll, Cleo Laine, Gordon Heath, and Brock Peters.

The Black Voices: On the Street in Watts. ALA Records ALA 1970 Stereo.

A Hand Is on the Gate. Verve Folkways FV–9040 OC 4s 12".

The Last Poets. Douglas Recording Corporation. Douglas 3 (1970). Produced by East Wind Associates. Distributed by Pip Records. Obiodun Oyewole, Alafia Pudim, Omar Ben Hassen reading their poems. Nilaja on percussion.

The Last Poets. The Original Last Poets from the Hit Movie "Right On." Juggernaut Records JUG–ST/LP 8802. David Nelson, Felipe Luciano, and Gylan Kain reading their poems.

The Last Poets. This is Madness. Douglas Communications Stereo ZO583.

Negro Folk Music of Africa and America. Folkways Records FE4500 4s 12".

New Jazz Poets. Edited by Walter Lowenfels. AR Records BR461.

Poetry of the Negro. Glory GLP–1 2s 12". Read by Sidney Poitier and Doris Belack.

Sidney Poitier Reads Poetry of the Black Man: With Doris Belack. United Artists Records UAS6693.

Songs of the American Negro Slaves. Folkways Records FD5252.

Spectrum in Black: Poems by 20th Century Black Poets. Scott, Foresman and Company 4149 4s 12″.

Spoken Arts Treasury of 100 Modern American Poets Reading Their Poems. SA—P—18. 18 volumes: James Weldon Johnson, v.1; Langston Hughes, v.7; Countee Cullen, v.8; Owen Dodson, v.12; Gwendolyn Brooks, v.13.

Today's Poets. Volume 4. Scholastic Records FS11004. Robert Hayden is included in this record.

Tough Poems for Tough People. Caedmon Records, Inc. (1971). Includes poems by Don L. Lee, Etheridge Knight, and other people.

Walk Together Children: The Black Scene in Prose, Poetry, and Song. Spoken Arts SA1030 4s 12″. 2 vol. Read and sung by Vinie Burrows.

Single Poets

Amini, Johari (Jewel Latimore) (see *Spectrum in Black*)

Angelou, Maya. *The Poetry of Maya Angelou.* GWP Records ST2001.

Baraka, Imamu Amiri. (see Jones, LeRoi)

Brooks, Gwendolyn. *Gwendolyn Brooks Reading Her Poetry: With an Introductory Poem by Don L. Lee.* Caedmon TC 1244. See also *Spoken Arts Treasury; Anthology of Negro Poets; A Hand Is on the Gate; Poetry of the Negro; Sidney Poitier Reads Poetry of the Black Man.*

Brown, Sterling. *The Dixie Belle. Sterling Brown and Langston Hughes Reading from Their Works.* Folkways Records, 1967. See also *Anthology of Negro Poets; A Hand Is on the Gate.*

Burroughs, Margaret G. *What Shall I Tell My Children, Who Are Black?* Sound-a-Rama SOR101 2s 12″.

Cullen, Countee. See *Spoken Arts Treasury; Anthology of Negro Poets; A Hand Is on the Gate; Poetry of the Negro; Sidney Poitier Reads Poetry of the Black Man.*

Danner, Margaret. See Hughes, Langston, *Writers of the Revolution*.

Dodson, Owen. *The Dream Awake*. Spoken Arts SA1095. See also *Spoken Arts Treasury*.

Dunbar, Paul Laurence. See *A Hand Is on the Gate; Walk Together Children*, volume 1; *Sidney Poitier Reads Poetry of the Black Man; Anthology of Negro Poets in the U.S.A.*

Giovanni, Nikki. *Truth Is on Its Way*. Saram, Inc. (1971).

Hayden, Robert. See *Today's Poets; Spectrum in Black*.

Henderson, David. See *New Jazz Poets*.

Hernton, Calvin C. See *New Jazz Poets*.

Hughes, Langston. *The Dream Keeper and Other Poems*. Folkways Records FP 104 2s 10". Read by the author. See also *Spoken Arts Treasury*; Brown Sterling. *The Dixie Belle; Anthology of Negro Poets; A Hand Is on the Gate; Poetry of the Negro; Sidney Poitier Reads Poetry of the Black Man*.

———. *Langston Hughes Reads and Talks about His Poems*. Spoken Arts SA 1064.

———. *The Poetry of Langston Hughes*. Caedmon (1968).

———. *Ruby Dee and Ossie Davis Read from Selected Poems of Langston Hughes* VTC 1272 (S–M).

Hughes, Langston, and Danner, Margaret. *Writers of the Revolution*. Black Forum BB 453.

Johnson, James Weldon. *God's Trombones*. Folkways Records FL 9788. Read by Bryce Bond. See also *Spoken Arts Treasury; Sidney Poitier Reads Poetry of the Black Man*.

Johnson, Joe. See *New Jazz Poets*.

Johnston, Percy E. See *New Jazz Poets*.

Jones, LeRoi. *Black & Beautiful . . . . Soul & Madness*. Jihad Productions. Jihad 1001.

———. *Sonny's Time Now*. Jihad Productions. Jihad 663.

Latimore, Jewel. See Amini, Johari.

Lee, Don L. *Rappin' & Readin'*. Broadside Voices LP–BR–1.

McKay, Claude. See *Anthology of Negro Poets; Anthology of Negro Poets in the U.S.A.; Spectrum in Black*.

Pritchard, Norman. See *New Jazz Poets*.

Reed, Ishmael. See *New Jazz Poets*.

Roberts, M. Younger. *A Reconstruction of a Me. A Letter to a Cold Place*. Red Dust, Inc. Red Dust 1.

Rodgers, Carolyn. See *Spectrum in Black*.

Scott-Heron, Gil. *Small Talk at 125th and Lenox*. Flying Dutchman Productions, Ltd. FDS–131.

Stone, Ronald. See *New Jazz Poets*.

Walker, Margaret. See *Anthology of Negro Poets; A Hand Is on the Gate*.

Wright, Richard. See *A Hand Is on the Gate; Walk Together Children; Spectrum in Black*.

TAPES

Collection

Broadside on Broadway: Seven Poets Read. Broadside Voices.* Casette. 1970. Dudley Randall, Jerry Whittington, Frenchy Hodges, Sonia Sanchez, Gwendolyn Brooks, Don L. Lee, and Margaret Walker read their poems.

Single Poets

Arnez, Nancy L. See Murphy, Beatrice M.

Bontemps, Arna. Library of Congress.** 98 LWO 4016. Tape. Reading his poems with commentary at Radio Station, WPLN, Nashville Public Library, May 22, 1963.

Brooks, Gwendolyn. *Gwendolyn Brooks Reads Family Pictures*. Broadside Voices. 5-inch reel. 7½ i.p.s.

———. Library of Congress. 109 LWO 3237. Tape. Reading her poems with comment, January 19, 1961.

Brooks, Gwendolyn, and Viereck, Peter. Library of Congress. 110 LWO 2863, reel 2. A joint reading by the two poets at the YMHA Poetry Center, New York City.

Dodson, Owen. Library of Congress. 199 LWO 3212. Tape. Reading his poems with comment, December 13, 1960.

Eckels, Jon. *Jon Eckels Reads Home Is Where the Soul Is*. Broadside Voices. 5-inch reel. 7½ i.p.s.

———. *Jon Eckels Reads Our Business in the Streets*. Broadside Voices. 5-inch reel. 3¾ i.p.s.

Emanuel, James A. *James Emanuel Reads Panther Man*. Broadside Voices. Casette and 5-inch reel. 3¾ i.p.s.

---

* Broadside Voices, 15205 Livernois, Detroit, Mich. 48238.
** Library of Congress, Recorded Sound Section, Washington, D.C. 20540.

————. *James Emanuel Reads The Treehouse and Other Poems*. Broadside Voices. 5-inch reel. 7½ i.p.s.

Giovanni, Nikki. *Nikki Giovanni Reads Re: Creation*. Broadside Voices. 5-inch reel. 3¾ i.p.s.

Harper, Michael. *History Is Your Own Heartbeat*. Urbana, The University of Illinois Press, 1971. Casette. Read by the poet.

Hughes, Langston. Library of Congress. 364 LWO 2838. Tape. Reading his poems with commentary, May 1, 1959.

————. Library of Congress. 365 LWO 3993, reel 3, side A. Tape. Guest on Florence Becker Lennon's program "Enjoyment of Poetry," broadcast January 18, 1959. They discuss "Poetry of the Blues."

Jeffers, Lance. *Lance Jeffers Reads My Blackness Is the Beauty of This Land*. Broadside Voices. 5-inch reel. 3¾ i.p.s.

Jones, LeRoi. Library of Congress. 391 LWO 2831. Tape. Reading his poems with commentary, April 17, 1959.

Kgositsile, Keorapetse. *Keorapetse Kgositsile Reads Spirits Unchained*. Broadside Voices. 5-inch reel. 7½ i.p.s.

Knight, Etheridge. *Etheridge Knights Reads Poems from Prison*. Broadside Voices. 5-inch reel. 3¾ i.p.s.

Lee, Don L. *Don L. Lee Reads Don't Cry, Scream*. Broadside Voices. 5-inch reel. 3¾ i.p.s.

————. *Don L. Lee Reads We Walk the Way of the New World*. Broadside Voices. 5-inch reel. 3¾ i.p.s.

Marvin X. *Marvin X Reads Black Man Listen*. Broadside Voices. 5-inch reel. 3¾ i.p.s.

Murphy, Beatrice M. and Arnez, Nancy L. *Beatrice Murphy and Nancy Arnez Read The Rocks Cry Out*. Broadside Voices. 5-inch reel. 7½ i.p.s.

Randall, Dudley. *Dudley Randall Reads Cities Burning*. Broadside Voices. 5-inch reel. 7½ i.p.s.

Sanchez, Sonia. *Sonia Sanchez Reads Homecoming*. Broadside Voices. 5-inch reel. 7½ i.p.s.

————. *Sonia Sanchez Reads We a BaddDDD People*. Broadside Voices. 5-inch reel. 3¾ i.p.s.

Stephany. *Stephany Reads Moving Deep*. Broadside Voices. 5-inch reel. 3¾ i.p.s.

Walcott, Derek. Library of Congress. 794 LWO 4363. Tape. Reading his poems with commentary, October 20, 1964.

Walker, Margaret. *Margaret Walker Reads Prophets for a New Day*. Broadside Voices. 5-inch reel. 3¾ i.p.s.

VIDEO TAPES

Knight, Etheridge. *Etheridge Knight Reads at Wayne State University*. 12/3/70. #48–A–B. Black and white. 50 minutes. Rental. Community Learning Center, 85 W. Canfield, Detroit, Mich. 48201.

La Grone, Oliver. *Oliver La Grone* (working in studio and reading his poetry). 35 minutes. Rental. Barry College, Miami, Fla. 33161.

Lee, Don L. *Don L. Lee Reads at Martin Luther King High School*. 7/23/70. #37. Black and white. Rental. Community Learning Center, 85 W. Canfield, Detroit, Mich. 48201.

Madgett, Naomi. *Naomi Madgett, Donald Hall, and Dan Gerber Reading Their Poems and Talking to Students*. Michigan Council for the Arts, 10125 E. Jefferson Ave., Detroit, Mich. 48214.

Poets Reading Their Poetry for OCC-TV. Robert Hayden, Naomi Madgett, and Dudley Randall Read the Six Poems They Want to Be Remembered By. 8mm. Black and white. 50 minutes. Rental. Oakland Community College. Orchard Lake, Mich. 48030.

Randall, Dudley. *Dudley Randall Reading and Discussing His Poetry for OCC-TV*. Black and white. 50 minutes. Rental. Oakland Community College. Orchard Lake, Mich. 48030.

FILMS

Gwendolyn Brooks. 16mm. 30 minutes. Black and white. Sale $125. Rental $6.75. 1967. Produced by WTTW, Chicago, Illinois. Indiana University, Audio-Visual Center. Bloomington, Indiana 47401.

Ridn and Stridn. Reachn and Teachn. A film showing Gwendolyn Brooks teaching in Chicago. Produced by Roy Lewis. 16mm. 30 minutes. Black and white. Rental. 206 N. La Porte Ave., South Bend, Ind. 46616.

Right On. Leacock-Pennebaker release of Woodie King, Jr. Features Gylan Kain, David Nelson, and Felipe Luciano. Directed by Herbert Danska. 16mm. Rental. Leacock Pennebaker, Inc., 56 West 45th St., New York, N.Y. 10036.

ABOUT THE EDITOR

DUDLEY RANDALL is an outstanding Black poet in his own right. He is director of the *Broadside Press*, and visiting professor of Black poetry at the University of Michigan.

DISCOVER
THE DRAMA OF LIFE
IN THE LIFE OF DRAMA

START A COLLECTION

With Bantam's fiction anthologies. you can begin almost anywhere. Choose from science fiction, classic literature, modern short stories, mythology. and more—all by both new and established writers in America and around the world.

Special Offer
Buy a Bantam Book
for only 50¢.

Now you can have Bantam's catalog filled with hundreds of titles plus take advantage of our unique and exciting bonus book offer. A special offer which gives you the opportunity to purchase a Bantam book for only 50¢. Here's how!

By ordering any five books at the regular price per order, you can also choose any other single book listed (up to a $5.95 value) for just 50¢. Some restrictions do apply, but for further details why not send for Bantam's catalog of titles today!

Just send us your name and address and we will send you a catalog!

BANTAM BOOKS, INC.
P.O. Box 1006, South Holland, Ill. 60473

Mr./Mrs./Ms. _____
(please print)

Address _____

City _____ State _____ Zip _____
FC(A)—10/87
Please allow four to six weeks for delivery.